A Passion for This Earth

A Passion
for This Earth

EXPLORING A NEW PARTNERSHIP OF
MAN, WOMAN & NATURE

———————— ————————

VALERIE ANDREWS

 HarperSanFrancisco
A Division of HarperCollins*Publishers*

Credits for quoted material and illustrations begin on p. 245

FIRST EDITION

Library of Congress Cataloging-in-Publication Data

Andrews, Valerie.
  A passion for this earth : exploring a new partnership of man, woman & nature / Valerie Andrews—1st ed.
     p.   cm.
  Includes bibliographical references.
  ISBN 0–06–250068–6
  1. Nature—Psychological aspects. 2. Mythology—Psychological aspects. 3. Ritual. I. Title.
  BF353.5.N37A53   1990
  304.2—dc20   89–46447
                                                    CIP

90   91   92   93   94   FAIR   10   9   8   7   6   5   4   3   2   1

This edition is printed on acid-free paper that meets the American National Standards Institute Z39.48 Standard.

For Laurance, Thomas, and Stephen

CONTENTS

ACKNOWLEDGMENTS

———————— ✿ ————————

My marriage to Stephen Yarabek and my daily life in a 1790 stone farmhouse in the Hudson River Valley have been invaluable preparation for the writing of this book. I am also grateful to my friend Thomas Berry, author of *The Dream of the Earth*, and to the Jungian analysts Marion Woodman and Robert Johnson for their work on masculine and feminine ways of being in the world. I am further indebted to the late Joseph Campbell, whose lectures have inspired my final section on mythology.

The following friends responded to the manuscript, offering valuable suggestions at different points along the way: Jean Shinoda Bolen, Sally Keil, Karla Knight, Rockwell Stensrud, Roger Robinson, Janet Hubbard-Brown, Diana Richardson, Rebecca Bogart, and Nancy Glickman. My editors at Harper & Row, Tom Grady and Michael Toms, believed in this book, knowing that it would touch on a wide variety of subjects—natural philosophy, religion, storytelling, and psychology. Laurance Rockefeller believed in me and made it possible for me to spend three years preparing these essays. Finally I would like to thank Mark Salzwedel, Karen Knight, Sam Keen, Dr. Robert Wallis, Laurie Winfrey, and Ned Leavitt, of the William Morris Agency.

INTRODUCTION

A human life, so often likened to a spectacle upon a stage, is more justly a ritual. The ancient values of dignity, beauty and poetry which sustain it are of Nature's inspiration; they are born of the mystery and beauty of the world.

—Henry Beston
The Outermost House

MANY TIMES I WONDERED IF I WERE MEANT TO be here on this earth or if I had landed here by chance, a random gesture of the cosmos, a speck in the wave of Brownian motion that is the living universe. Though I longed to feel a part of all creation, it seemed as though I were standing outside it, viewing nature as I would a diorama, a neatly packaged piece of history that my culture had forgotten and outgrown. Several years ago, while editing a journal inspired by the anthropologist Margaret Mead, I discovered that many of my contemporaries also suffered from this feeling of rootlessness and alienation. Indeed, my generation seemed to have lost its sense of balance and belonging as we lost our daily contact with the land. With this in mind, I planned an issue of the journal that would ask, "What inner stability do we receive from living closer to nature? What is so important about simply being where we are?"

To answer these questions I began to explore my own adopted territory—the Hudson River Valley—with the help of Stephen Yarabek, a landscape architect and environmental planner. Stephen introduced me to a world I never knew existed just twenty five miles north of New York City—one populated by wildflowers and weeping beeches, eagles and hawks, streams and hidden springs. One day as we toured the Tarrytown hills, I came upon a stand of trees that recalled my childhood hideaway. As a young girl, I went to a similar clearing in the woods, knelt down on the soft earth, and thanked the land for nourishing and sustaining me. Now when I beheld this familiar scene, I put my arms around a nearby oak and felt an overwhelming sense of grief. I had known my place in the world with the innate wisdom of a child, but at some point, I had refused to love the earth because I did not want to face the pain of losing it again.

Five years ago, I married Stephen and moved to the foothills of the Catskill Mountains in upstate New York. We bought an old farmhouse nestled in the woods along the Rondout Creek and were welcomed by a great blue heron and sixteen white-tailed deer. In these new surroundings, I found a safe haven from which to meditate on the loss of place my entire generation had endured.

By the 1960s my childhood landscape was gone forever, buried beneath the tarmac of a suburban road. The two-hundred-year-old oak, the grove of paper birches, the apple orchard, the hedgerows, and the open fields had all disappeared. In just two decades, nature had become "quaint" and wilderness a weekend luxury. This was not an isolated problem; other regions of the country witnessed a construction boom that threatened to make nature a relic of the past. Rural pastures and rolling hills gave way to malls and major highways, and the history and character of America began to fade away as well. I believe this loss of place has damaged us in ways we have yet to understand, and that is why the first part of this book is called "Facing the Wound."

The land is the key to our inner nature, its beauty and its violence but a mirror of the light and shadow in the human soul. Landscape, then, is a revelation of the Self and a key to our own moods and inner changes. "Each landscape asks the same question," says the novelist Laurence Durrell. "I am watching myself in you—are you watching yourself in me?" The earth contains a blueprint of the human psyche, a map of our innate character. It is as accurate an indicator of who we are as the narrow-ribboned chromosomes that determine our intelligence and genetic sensitivities. Durrell tells an intriguing story about a group of Chinese immigrants who came to San Francisco in the 1940s. Within the space of two generations, this group had ceased to look like "homegrown" Chinese. He is quick to point out that the people did not intermarry. Instead, they were transformed by the land, which exerts its own kind of magnetic pull upon the body and the spirit. This story reminds us that there is a profound relation between the human and the earth and that we are transformed by a continual exchange of energies.

The early chapters of this book offer a prescription of sorts: They call on us to reinstate our dialogue with nature, for when we ignore the living world, we lose a portion of ourselves. The health of the person is linked to the well-being of the planet, and there can be no change in the body of the world without a corresponding change in us. This century has given us many images of our shared distress. We have only to juxtapose Giacometti's haunting sculpture of "the human forest" and a dying woodland to see the profound resemblance between our withered bodies and the starvation of the earth itself (see figure 1). There is also an eerie similarity between human cancer cells and the welts carved into the landscape by an unrelenting drought (see figure 2). These striking patterns make clear that our own illnesses are echoed by the land and that there can be no separation of the wound within and the wound without.

---- ❀ ----

I have begun to think that the most threatening diseases of our time, such as AIDS and cancer, are indications that we are living out of phase with the larger cycles of this planet. How can we be at ease within the human body if we no longer feel bound and held by matter, if we no longer have a sense of being *in* and *of* the world?

Fig. 1 *The anorexic earth: a withered forest in Hawaii* (left) *and Giacometti's 1950 portrayal of the human forest.*

 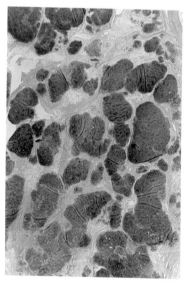

Fig. 2 *Cancer and the planet: excess radiation affects the earth* (left) *and also changes bone marrow in the human body.*

I learned about this correspondence firsthand when a series of infections paralyzed my immune system for a period of four years. As a journalist, I pushed myself well beyond my limits, putting in fourteen hours a day with no time out for renewal. Finally, I had to pay the price for ignoring one of nature's basic laws.

My healing came, slowly, as I became a chronicler of wildlife on the Rondout Creek. At dawn I watched sixteen white-tailed deer cross the Rondout in a shroud of morning fog. Then I would sit on the banks with my tea as the great blue heron flew above me. Later I walked to a nearby meadow to gather chicory and Queen Anne's lace. On the days I felt strong, I rowed out into the middle of the creek to watch the muskrats build their sandy burrows near the shore. In winter, I saw ice floes form like giant vertebrae along the white spine of the river. And in the spring, I witnessed the wavelike migrations of the shad and carp. As I lived through the changing of the seasons, I began to see myself in a different context. I no longer worried about the demands of a job or a corporation. Instead, I was absorbed in the life cycle of an estuary.

In the quiet time so necessary for my recovery, I began to read about early matriarchal cultures that worshiped the earth as a goddess, "the Great Mother" who gives birth to all creation. In religious ceremonies, supplicants went down into a cave or labyrinth to renew their contact with the land. We would do well to remember that the word *earth* comes from the same Indo-European root that gives us *humus* and *humility*. Honoring our connection to the earth, then, is a way of humbling ourselves, and an antidote for the inflated spirit of our times. "The sky's the limit," we say, as we pledge ourselves to an upward spiral of achievement. Yet these older rites provide us with a different kind of knowledge. They tell us that we must go "downward and inward" and reenact the journey of the seed.

The stories of Inanna and Persephone were helpful to me, for they explained how we can turn inward and discover our own "seed nature." From these, I learned that the human is subject to the same pattern of growth and transformation that guides the natural world. Like all other living things, we must make our descent into the darkness then wait for some new kind of wisdom to take root. The second part of this book, "Rituals of Completion," shows how we participate in this universal drama of resurrection and rebirth.

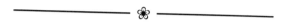

I believe that, over time, we must move toward the sacred marriage—a state where men and women are equal partners and act as loving stewards of the earth. This is the subject of my final section, "Toward a New Mythology."

Every culture gains its inspiration from a story and for the last two thousand years we have been guided by Greek tales of heroism and adventure. The hero myth tells us about the pain and suffering required to achieve our individuality—yet it tells us precious little about the compassion we need to have for one another and for the living world. We are not meant to live solely in the heroic mode; another kind of story is also necessary—one that helps us find our place within the body of the earth. Where can we turn for this model of relationship? Fortunately, the unity of man, woman, and nature appears as a main theme in the legends of the Celts. In this tradition, the king is wedded to the land just as surely as he is wedded to his wife, and every marriage must reflect this deep ecology. In this body of literature, relationship is aimed not at personal gain and satisfaction but at the preservation of all life.

Can the sacred marriage celebrated in early agrarian societies still be an inspiration for us in modern times? I believe it can, if we look at it primarily as an attitude, as a way of being on this earth. While we no longer depend so directly on the land for our livelihood, the earth still shapes our passions and our creativity. We are nevertheless part of a grand plan, and as the poet Wendell Berry tells us,

> Marriages to marriages are joined,
> husband and wife
> are plighted
> to all husbands and wives.
> Any life has all lives for its delight.

The southern writer Carson McCullers speaks of this bond in one of her short stories. She suggests that we learn to love the simple things in nature before we learn to care for one another. She then proposes a hierarchy of relationship: first you love a rock, then a cloud, then a tree, and your abilities will grow until one day you are ready to love a human being.

Marriage, then, is not something that takes place between two people; it is the culmination of all our earthly histories. Our love for one another is supported by the world itself and we receive one another in the same way that we embrace the mountains, lakes, and trees. Perhaps our true vocation lies in this kind of remembering.

Over the last few years, I have been engaged in one long ritual of returning to the earth. I began by acknowledging how our institutions and relationships have been damaged in our retreat from nature. Economics, which once was rooted in the seasons, has now become disembodied and abstract. Our organizations are static and unchanging. And our Information Culture only gives us half the picture since it still fails to take into account the spontaneity of life. At such times, we are thrown back on our own resources and forced to rediscover the meaning of nature in and for ourselves.

Though we live in a difficult period of transition, there is still the possibility of awe and wonder. Indeed, that is what the remaining essays are about. With a new and different orientation, I believe that we can move from the wound to the unifying vision. As we begin to honor the partnership of man, woman, and the earth, we will know the truth inherent in the poet's words:

> The way I go
> is marriage to this place
> grace beyond chance,
> love's braided dance
> covering the world.

Valerie Andrews
OLD HURLEY, NEW YORK
APRIL 1990

ONE

Facing the Wound

BEGINNING WITH A PLACE

What is important is the moment of opening a life and feeling it touch our present world.

—Annie Dillard
An American Childhood

As A CHILD I HAD A SECRET PLACE. EVERY DAY AT sunset I visited a grove of birch trees surrounded by a hedge of sweet-smelling privet. At the center was a mound where I would lie down and listen to the steady rhythmic heartbeat of the earth. For seven years I performed this daily ritual; even in winter I could feel this pulse as though I were connected by a rootlike umbilicus to the dark core of the land.

The grove faced west and formed a kind of *kiva* or womblike container. This enclosure had all the power of an ancient shrine; it was a place of dying and becoming. As the light intensified and left the sky awash in crimson flames, I learned a way of being in the world and in transition. Something within me changed as the earth underwent its own transfiguration and as the day's activity gave way to the long, slow respiration of the night.

This is how, at the beginning of my life, I received my teachings directly from the natural world. I understood the rhythm of existence through the interplay of light and shadow and the subtle changes of the air and climate. I learned that for every mood there is a corresponding season and that our lives are seamlessly connected to the great life of the earth. When I withdrew in winter and found myself in dark and inaccessible regions, I came to know that darkness is a time for the migration of the soul; I saw then what we hold in common with the roots and seeds—a stage of mute and invisible growth. My inner changes and emotions were often triggered by the land: I would feel the breakthrough of the spring as the windswept sky and a sudden movement of the clouds brought forth a new round of activity. I would become like the hard, insistent shoots sprouting upward from the earth, and something in me would be heartened and encouraged as I stretched my spirit toward the light. The eruptions of the crocus and the daffodil still remind me that in the days ahead I will know the exhilaration of opening that belongs to the buds and flowers. By such observations, we discover that life is not static or fixed; one thing flows into the next, and we are standing in the midst of it wide-eyed and innocent.

There is, and will forever be, a link between the guilelessness of childhood and the revelation of the land. This is what allows us to perceive the magic of creation. We remain under its spell until the onset of adulthood; then so often the bond is broken, the intimacy lost, as we surrender to a world of our own making, a world where everything is quantified and known. The poet Sven Birkerts describes the dual loss of childhood and nature in this way:

> I had a happy childhood. That's what I say now. Back then it was not one thing or another, just a way things had of happening, natural and unquestioned, waking up and going about the daily business. I see now that I was full to the brim, with nothing lacking; that space and time were not yet separable concepts at all. "Weren't you ever bored?" Dear God, I was in an ecstacy of boredom! I was so bored that time would back up on itself and start flowing in a new direction. And yet it wasn't like the trivial boredom which afflicts me now. It was a dream, a plenitude. The whole of my childhood was innoculated with it. Boredom: mother of absorption . . . combustions of fantasy, riotous private ritual.
>
> Nowadays I catch myself regarding some particular landscape as if it were possessed of passive sen-

tience. Have I become more spiritually attuned? Or
is it simply that landscape itself has become an em-
blem of the timeless perception of childhood?
Could it be that the living otherness I sense is nothing more than the self I had to bury?

I believe that our souls are formed in the idleness of youth,
and it is then, when our time is unstructured and unmeasured,
that we know ourselves to be at one with the essential wisdom
of the world. When I was seven, I roamed the hillsides and the
meadows, aware that the world around me was engaged in an
endless cycle of renewal. I went to my birch grove, certain that
the land would accept all my loves and disappointments and
receive my childhood joys and tragedies as it received all other
living things. It was the earth that gave me my first sense of
communion and, like Birkerts, I felt that my best, my truest self
was connected to a few square miles of land.

When I was twelve, my family moved from the country to
the crowded suburbs of New Jersey, and I felt we had done the
unforgiveable—we had left behind the place that supported us
and gave us everlasting life. There were no more rose bushes or
rows of irises and hollyhocks. I could no longer pick apples
from our yard or run down the road to get fresh eggs from the
neighbor's farm.

Years later, I realized that the land is always with us. The
world as we first knew it remains imprinted on the body and
the brain like tiny fossils embedded in a piece of shale. As a
child, one has that magical capacity to move among the many
eras of the earth; to see the land as an animal does; to experience the sky from the perspective of a flower or a bee; to feel
the earth quiver and breathe beneath us; to know a hundred
different smells of mud and listen unself-consciously to the
soughing of the trees. We are continually articulating the intelligence of the planet, which has grown up through all the species. The whole earth lives within us, and in every moment, we
are both its creators and discoverers. We only need to reawaken
all these early memories.

———————————— ❧ ————————————

Our first picture of the world contributes, in a major way, to the formation of our identity. In *An American Childhood,* Annie Dillard talks about the "inner" meaning of geography:

> Walking was my project before reading. The text I read was the town; the book I made up was a map. First I had walked across one of our sideyards to the blackened alley and [found] a buried dime. Now I walked to piano lessons, four long blocks north of school and three zigzag blocks, into an Irish neighborhood near Thomas Boulevard. . . .
>
> I pushed at my map's edges. Alone at night I added newly memorized streets and blocks to old streets and clocks, and imagined connecting them on foot. From my parent's earlier injunctions I felt that my life depended on keeping it all straight— remembering where on earth I lived.

The land is truly the larger body that contains us; it is our second skin. How far do I venture? What passage do I find scary? What streets and hills are safe? In childhood, the body of the earth is like a second mother; we push ourselves against it as an infant cranes and pushes outward from the breast, exploring its own strength and testing human boundaries.

Like Dillard, I was a wanderer. I walked down the blue slate path to Union Avenue to buy forbidden strands of shoestring candy. I ambled down the gravel road to an abandoned quarry where I jammed my pockets full of granite and rose quartz. I pushed my way through the hedgerow by the chicken farm to explore an abandoned coop, then made my way across the fields to jump onto the back of a skittish Palomino horse. With each daring step, I came to know the world as my intimate. In  all, I gained from the land around my home the most important gift: a sense of constancy.

Several years ago, I discovered a New England artist who translated this dynamic into a playground sculpture. He fashioned a reclining woman out of sod, and the children clambered up two mounds that were her breasts, hugged her huge torso, and jumped from her wide hips. This "earth mother" accomplished what initiation rites once did in the past, encouraging these young people to move, at their own pace, away from the body of the parent to forge a new relation with the body of the world.

I often wonder how children who live in cities and high-rise apartment buildings begin to know such things. How do they discover that they, too, are supported by the earth? As I look back, I see that the land met me with a fidelity that was difficult for any single person to achieve. As a child, I turned to the meadows and the trees, aware that there were two kinds of nurturing: while my parents provided me with human comforts, this place introduced me to the energies of life.

My early bond with nature has saved me from despair and resignation in the worst of times. When frightened or confused, there was always something to fall back on—an experience of the world as self-renewing, a knowledge that each phase is only temporary, and a belief in the alternating pattern of loss and reconciliation that is at the core of our existence.

When young people no longer have access to nature, they do not have the information they need to nourish and sustain themselves in a changing world. Consider the disturbing case of Cobb County, Georgia. Fifteen years ago, it was one big open pasture. Yet now it is a patchwork of suburban towns. The population has climbed to over half a million, and at the same time, the teenage suicide rate has soared to over fifty in a single year. A local psychiatrist explained that the young people had great difficulty dealing with the region's fast development. "You're going to have this kind of turmoil," he warned, "wherever you have greater instability and less tradition." There are many more Cobb counties in America, and many more young people suffer from a similar kind of rootlessness. How long before we realize that the human spirit is and must be rooted in the land?

The trouble is we Americans tend to disregard the landscape, to build on it willy-nilly, and use it for a variety of ends not at all related to the spirit of the place. A nation of immigrants, we have no feeling for the timeworn and the permanent. For us, the goal is leaving home, not standing by it and enhancing it. In an interview with the Paris magazine *L'Autre Journal*, François Mitterand criticized us for this failing. "The American spirit is fired by the journey, the adventure, the departure—by this need to escape, to go wherever your steps lead, to get away. From what? From convention, from home. Maybe—who knows?—from oneself, from death. One is looking for a better world and that inevitably lies beyond the horizon. So one keeps walking as long as there's hope. What society could fulfill this aspiration? None. It is a metaphysical quest and politics provides no answer of this kind."

Part of the problem is that America became a nation long before it had the chance to know itself as *a land*. When the French, the English, and the Dutch came to this continent, they brought their own customs and cultural traditions, ignoring the Native Americans who had a deeper understanding of this earth. Our ancestors believed they had a right to impose their European values wherever they settled down, and as a result, we have yet to realize how we are shaped by a given region, how our character is formed by simply being where we are.

Americans faced another major round of dislocations in the first half of this century as they left their farms for the factories and began to forge a culture totally removed from the dictates of the land. The Kentucky poet and essayist Wendell Berry said, "In the old days you didn't go to school to study agriculture. You knew that every nook and cranny of a field was different, and so you spent a lifetime trying to get to know a single farm." By the 1940s, however, everyone had forgotten the particulars. Local cycles all blended into one national myth of steady growth. By the postwar era, it was patriotic to consume, one's national duty to spend and bolster the economy.

My parents left a small town in upstate New York and experienced this national conversion from scarcity to affluence. In their lifetimes, our culture went from deprivation to repeated gorging. I have a photograph of them standing on the porch of my grandfather's stone house in Port Dickinson, near Binghamton, in 1934. My mother and father are dressed in second-hand overcoats that hang upon their slender frames like medieval cassocks. Twenty years later, things have changed considerably. Another snapshot shows my mother in a wool crepe suit with matching hat and shoes and father in a double-breasted tweed and gray fedora. They are posed in front of their new Buick sedan at a fashionable resort along the Jersey shore. In the years that followed, they moved to twelve different cities, chasing the American Dream of affluence, never imagining that they would begin to suffer from a poverty of place.

Perhaps this generation was so eager to pack up and leave for any town that promised them a better living because they had already been uprooted—first by a depression and then by a major war. These two events had forced them into an unfamiliar territory with no hope of returning to a way of life they knew before. My father and his brothers left home in the 1930s when my grandfather lost his job. They went to France and the Pacific during the war, and afterward they moved to Alaska, California, Rhode Island, and New York. Through all this, my grandfather stayed behind, patiently filing all their letters according to the city postmark.

While my parents endured the loss of their old neighborhood, however, I grew up contemplating the loss of an entire world. During the height of the Cold War, my grade-school classes were interrupted by the shriek of air-raid sirens. With the other children, I was ushered into a dark corner of the basement and told to place my head between my knees—as if this simple gesture could protect us all from nuclear debris. I

crouched into this fetal pose, painfully aware of my own end-
ings and beginnings. It seemed that I had come into the world
in order to be pushed out of it, that I had learned to love this
place only to be reminded of its impending doom.

My generation experienced other major assaults upon its tender sensibilities. In the 1950s, city bureaucrats began to system-
atically destroy the architecture and the landscape that linked
us to a certain time and place. Critic Ada Louise Huxtable
described the loss of regional style and character that took
place in the last three decades, summing up the damage in a
single phrase: "Hello hamburger, goodbye history." Malls, fast-
food chains, and superhighways went up overnight, and our
open spaces suddenly were made into disconnected towns.

Then there was the phenomenon of moving. In the 1950s,
"company men" packed up their families every three or four
years to accommodate routine transfers and promotions. My
parents managed to outmaneuver even these statistics, and to
accommodate my father's business, we moved every two. By
the time I was thirty, I realized that I had unconsciously accepted this two-year exodus as the basic rhythm of my life. I
left home at age eighteen, transferred colleges twice, and lived
in six different apartments in the space of thirteen years. To
change this pattern, I had to grieve for all the childhood places
I had left behind. In the process, I realized that moving is a
major rite of passage that affects us just as deeply as the death
of a parent or a spouse. How, then, are we to mark the loss of
a community and begin to embrace another? The Welcome Wa-
gon, that American convention, is of little help; it introduces us
to the butcher and the baker, but it fails to introduce us to the
flow of life.

Today we are all obsessed with homelessness. Most of us
have never had to spend a night without food or shelter, yet as
we tiptoe by the sleeping bodies on sidewalks and park benches,
we feel that somehow we, too, are dispossessed. We have a
deepening sense of our own spiritual rootlessness, and this has
brought out a new morbidity in the American psyche. Holly-

wood has even picked up on our feeling of displacement. Steven Spielberg's E.T. is a homeless creature from another galaxy who reflects our many problems here on earth: The lovable alien manages to embody both the pathos of the displaced elderly and the anxiety of a lost child. Yet the secret of one of America's most popular movies is this: When E.T. longs for his mother planet, we long to be comforted ourselves.

As we baby boomers left behind the towns that gave us our original feeling of belonging, we grew accustomed to the repeated exodus. Our lives began with a series of postwar uprootings, and we tried to take our moves in stride. Then, by middle age, something unexpected happened: We began to long for some deeply buried, highly subjective fantasy of place. Garrison Keillor's *Lake Wobegon Days* became an instant best-seller because it provided us with a ready-made hometown. It gave us the sense of familiarity we craved, offering a litany of regressive sameness, a compensation for our hyperactive lives. In Lake Wobegon, things happen at a nearly hypnotizing pace: Florian Krebsbach drives a '66 Chevy with only forty-two thousand miles on it. Each turn of his life is taken in slow motion, and he never wanders very far from town. This deliberate pace seems to satisfy him, for when he looks at Main Street and at his wife, "he sees them brand-new like his car." Small-town life seems to retard the flow of time: People are born and grow up through the awkward stages. They marry, grow old, and die. Yet in Lake Wobegon, all this happens with so little drama and dissension. Life does not come in spurts and jumps; it is more like an underground stream; the currents are hidden, and the most important things take place out of sight. The main events are not discussed and analyzed; instead, they are gently worn and put away.

By the end of the tale, however, this fantasy of ease and timelessness is broken. Lake Wobegon's children gradually leave home, just like the rest of us. Some thirty years later, they lie in bed at night and think of the price they've had to pay for their constant journeying:

"I am forty-three years old," says one displaced Wobegonian, "I haven't lived there for twenty-five years. I've lived in a series of eleven apartments and three houses, most within a few miles of each other in St. Paul and Minneapolis. Every couple of years the urge strikes to pack the books and unscrew the table legs and haul off to a new site. The mail is forwarded, sometimes from a house several stops back down the line, the front of the envelope covered with addresses, but friends are lost—most all the time, it's sad to think about it. All those long conversations in vanished kitchens when for an evening we achieved a perfect understanding that, no matter what happened, we were true comrades and our affection would endure, and now our friendship is gone to pieces and I can't account for it."

Sense of place is more than a Grant Wood painting of a midwestern hayfield or an Andrew Wyeth meadow on the outskirts of a small New England town. It encompasses a longing for home and for time-worn relationships. We are all looking for a safe harbor, and the question is, How will we go about creating it for ourselves?

When my husband and I first moved to the Rondout Creek, outside Kingston, New York, we wanted to hold a ceremony to celebrate our arrival in this place. As it happened, our property faced an island where the last Esopus Indian had set up camp. He had lived there until the early 1950s, canoeing into the village through the locks of the old Delaware and Hudson Canal. When he reached old age he built a bier from pine branches and simply lay down on the earth to die. We therefore decided it would be appropriate to acknowledge the Native American presence on this land.

The Omaha have an initiation rite that introduces a newborn child to nature. They believe we must be presented to the sun, moon, wind, and stars and to all the living creatures of the earth. This ritual shows a remarkable understanding of our reciprocity: The world needs to accept our human consciousness, while we, in turn, must pledge our lives to protect and honor its inhabitants. With the help of our friend the historian Thomas Berry, we came up with a version of this ceremony that would introduce us to the natural world. Twelve of us stood in a circle on the swelling banks of the Rondout after a new spring rain, and as the blue heron nestled on a nearby branch, Berry chanted these verses from the Omaha prayer:

> Ho! Ye Sun, Moon, Stars, all ye that move in the
> heavens,
> I bid you hear me!
> Into your midst has come a new life.
> Consent ye, I implore.
> Make its path smooth, that it may reach the brow
> of the first hill.
>
> Ho! Ye Winds, Clouds, Rain, Mist, all ye that move
> in the air,
> I bid you hear me!
> Into your midst has come a new life.
> Make its path smooth that it may reach the brow
> of the second hill.
>
> Ho! Ye Hills, Valleys, Rivers, Lakes, Trees, Grasses,
> all ye of the earth,
> I bid you hear me!
> Into your midst has come a new life.
> Make its path smooth that it may reach the brow
> of the third hill.
>
> Ho! Ye Birds, great and small, that fly in the air,
> Ho! Ye Animals, great and small, that dwell in the
> forest,
> Ho! Ye Insects that creep among the grasses and
> burrow in the ground,
> I bid you hear me!

Into your midst has come a new life.
Make its path smooth, that it may reach the brow
    of the fourth hill.

Ho! All ye of the heavens, all ye of the air,
    all ye of the earth;
I bid you all to hear me!
Into your midst has come a new life.
Consent ye, consent ye all, I implore
Make its path smooth—then shall it travel
    beyond the four hills!

We then took water from the Rondout and went inside to bless each room in the house. The emphasis was not on the building, however, as usual in a traditional American house-warming. Instead, the idea was to connect us to the many creatures with which we shared the riverbanks: to honor the muskrat and the beaver, the heron, and the deer. At the conclusion of this ceremony, we promised to actively serve and protect this special portion of the world.

Later that year I discovered that my ancestors had been among the early settlers along the Roudout Creek. The family of Jacob van Osterhoudt came here from Brabrant in the 1690s. Without realizing it, I had returned to the place my family settled three hundred years ago. This part of the Hudson valley with its stone houses, streams, and apple orchards seems so familiar to me that at times, I feel that I am remembering this place rather than discovering it. I have come to believe that the earth, too, has a collective memory and is trying to call us back to it. If so, then we are not here by accident but because we have been summoned by the spirit of the land.

When the Swiss psychoanalyst C. G. Jung visited the Pueblo Indians in the early 1950s, he was greatly impressed by Native Americans' feeling for human-earth relationship. In his book *Memories, Dreams, Reflections,* he describes a chance meeting with an elder of the tribe:

I stood by the river and looked up at the mountains. Suddenly a deep voice, vibrant with sup-

pressed emotion, spoke from behind me into my left
ear. "Do you not think all life comes from the
mountain?" An elderly Indian had come up to me,
inaudible in his moccasins, and had asked me this
heaven-knows how far-reaching question. [I
glanced] at the river pouring down from the mountain. Obviously all life came from the mountain for
where there is water, there is life. . . .

If for a moment we put away all European ra-
tionalism and transport ourselves in to the clear
mountain air of that solitary plateau; if we also set
aside our intimate knowledge of the world and exchange it for a horizon that seems immeasurable,
we will begin to achieve an inner comprehension of
the Pueblo Indian's point of view. "All life comes
from the mountain," is immediately convincing to
him and he is equally certain that he lives upon the
roof of an immeasurable world, closest to God. He,
above all others, has the Divinity's ear and his ritual
act will reach the distant sun soonest of all. . . .
Such a man is, in the fullest sense of the word, in
his proper place.

Native Americans have elaborate creation stories that center
the tribe in place and time. When a child is born, he or she
inherits this story; here the village is the center of the universe,
the family is "the first people," and their rituals the first ever
to be performed. Tribal cultures begin with a sense of wholeness
and the feeling that they are absolutely necessary in the round
of life. Yet in our films and our popular literature, we pass on
our tales of loss: loss of home, loss of land, loss of family, loss
of Self. Somewhere along the line, we trade our own tales of
unity for a Humpty-Dumpty shattering. Because we have no
creation stories, we stand like helpless children, watching as the
world around us breaks and splinters into many parts.

We need a new story now to help us endure the pain of many
separations—from parents and loved ones, from schools, jobs,
and whole communities. We long to feel that sense of unity the

poet Robert Duncan speaks of as the property of the earth
itself:

> Often I am permitted to return to a meadow
> as if it were a given property of the mind
> that holds certain bounds against chaos,
> that is a place of first permission,
> everlasting omen of what is.

We enter the meadow in the morning of creation, yet by
afternoon the unity is broken; we move from a secure grounding in the rhythms of the earth into a phase of loss and separation. The meadow recedes from us and takes its place in the
realm of memory and regret. Then as Duncan says,

> It is only a dream of the grass blowing
> east against the course of the sun
> in an hour before the sun's going down. . . .
> whose secret we see in a children's game
> of ring a round of roses told.

We want to feel at one with our surroundings, but it is hard
to do so when everything around us is being rearranged. The
intellectual explorations of the twentieth century have radically
changed our way of being in the world. The Cubist painters
took apart the visual world and reassembled it. Filmmakers
abandoned the dramatic narrative and began playing tricks
with memory. Joyce and Stein dissected human speech, and
with Shoenberg and Stravinsky, music became an unlyrical dis-
sent, a strange chromatic cry closing in upon itself with no
release.

Faced with this anarchy of perception, we began to compart-
mentalize the world around us; we put nature in parks, history
in museums, and animals in zoos. We even tried to fit life itself
into rigid categories. As Thomas Berry says, "Every discipline—
law, medicine, education, business and religion—became coun-
terproductive in its pursuit of knowledge. All lost sight of their

original purpose—to enhance the relation between the human and the earth."

In this new orientation, we have been cut off from the eros of the moment. We become obsessed with *buying in,* not *being in.* We have conquered the environment, and in our obsession for control, we no longer allow the environment to live in us. The American watercolorist James Fitzgerald left the harried life-style of the city to reclaim the timeless pleasures of the earth. In the 1950s, he took refuge on an island off the coast of Maine and noted in his diary: "Free the mind from the domination of time and everything takes on a curious beauty. Experience then seems to exist for its own sake with a flavor and a color and a fragrance it had not before. The scene is no longer blurred and streaming away from us, broken by an anxious heart."

To achieve a new appreciation of the living world, we are now in the awkward position of having to reverse the flow of energy. Our rationality has insulated us from nature and from the dark core of the human psyche. It has kept us from confronting the unpredictable and unknown. Significantly, this meeting with the nonrational is the goal of tribal teaching. Pueblo initiation consists of going down into a *kiva,* a womblike hole in the earth (see figure 3). Here, in the darkness, the individual seeks a confrontation with the archetypal powers of creation. There is no more important experience than this time when a young person goes into nature, voluntarily exposes himself or herself to danger, and prays for help from a spirit guide. Through this act, earth and spirit are aligned. Without it, the individual will fail at every task in life.

In *Respect for Life,* Kiowa elder Guy Quetone explains, "In order to get the spirit, you have to go to some lonely place. You

Fig. 3 *This ceremonial* kiva *in Mexico was built into a canyon floor during the eleventh century. Over the years, its mud-and-log roof has worn away. The round holes are tunnels where initiates descended into the earth.*

fast there for four days. Pray to Nature that he endow you with gifts. There's a big lake, Devil's Lake, where many men have gone to get that gift. Sometimes the water boils and roars and speaks and the test comes. If you get scared and run off, you don't get it. You have to hold your ground." This is something the modern world has yet to learn; we need to hold our ground and face the brooding powers of creation, for there is no growth without a confrontation of this archetype.

The novelist Carlos Fuentes reminds us of a universal correspondence between *terra,* the earth—and *terror.*

> . . . terror is the true state of all creatures. Terror, a
> state of substantive union with the earth, and a de-
> sire to withdraw forever from the earth.
> (*Terra Nostra*)

To live fully we must come to terms with this paradox: we long to enter the body of the earth and give ourselves to the abyss, yet an innate fear propels us away from these portentous depths. When I began to write this book, I decided to confront my own ambivalence toward nature, and so I spent a month in a beach house, near a wildlife sanctuary situated on the San Andreas fault. On my morning walks, I encountered seal and egret, and I watched the somber ceremonies of the hawks. This was the time of winter storms; the sea raged and each day new bones and fossils washed up on the shore. Once I found the mutilated body of a sea lion and the skeleton of a shark. A few weeks into the retreat I began to wake in the darkest hour of the night. My heart was pounding, and I felt surrounded by a nameless dread. My anxiety was so deep that there were no names or faces I could connect with it. Though I tried to relate this feeling to some particular event, it seemed that I had always carried this terror somewhere inside me.

My sleep was always interrupted at that mythic time between 4 and 5 A.M., known as the "Hour of the Wolf." In Nordic culture, this is the moment when the people fear that they will be devoured by the darkness and entombed in endless night. After a while, however, I began to realize that this was a universal terror. There was nothing I could do except be there with my fear and vulnerability. "Yes," I would say aloud to the pursuing terror, "I am awake and present," and then I would begin to address this feeling ritually. On dark nights, I would light a fire and stay close to the hearth. But when there was a moon, I would sit beneath an open window and watch the clouds as they swirled above the open sea. Usually I found myself praying, asking to be guided in the time when all creation was trying to cross over, to make the same transition from darkness into light.

As I watched the horizon, the sky began to shimmer. Then an embryonic shape began to twist and pull within the void. Moments later, dawn broke open like an egg. I was flooded with relief, and finally I fell back to sleep, exhausted from my vigil. I did not cease to wake at this hour of the night, however, until I had come to terms with my fear of the living world. By the end of the retreat, I knew I could stand my ground. The dark side of nature was not something from which to escape or hide; instead, it was a known protagonist.

Indian children raised according to the old traditions become stewards of the planet by the age of four. Pueblo elder Victor Sarracino describes in *Respect for Life* an important ceremony where "a circle of hair is cut from the center of a child's head— just like your monk's. There we attach an eagle feather and the child makes a pledge to protect forever all things of nature: the animals, the plants, the air, and all he comes in contact with." In tribal societies, young people are encouraged to feel their way into existence, to identify with the spirit in all living creatures. Such wisdom is a part of the entire culture; it is not relegated to the realm of religious teachings or considered apart from daily life.

Ironically, we are kept from a full meeting with nature by our spiritual traditions. Christianity has conditioned us to believe in the end of the world, and so we fail to ask the most important question: How do I come to terms with the energies of life? This problem is compounded by our schools and institutions, which do not teach us how to respect the natural world. Some time ago I talked with M.I.T. psychologist Sherry Turkle, author of *The Second Self: Computers and the Human Spirit,* about some disturbing changes in our self-perception. Turkle says that the computer is now the main carrier of our psychological projections, an important yardstick against which we measure our own talents and abilities. There was once a time when such projections were safely carried by nature—children used to identify their moods and feelings with changes in the land or in the seasons and learn about their own potential by studying some aspect of animal life. Now, Turkle believes, our children tend to find their own reflection in machines. One day she followed a fourth-grader away from the computer and found him in the corner of a school yard, killing ants.

> "Why are you doing that?" she asked.
> "They're not alive," the boy explained. "So it's okay to crush them."
> "But how do you know?"
> "Because they do not *think*."

This dialogue is chilling, for it shows that many of us believe the ability to reason gives us life. Our whole society is enmeshed in computer rationality, and many of our colloquialisms are taken directly from this subculture. If someone annoys us, we say, "They do not count." When something does not work, we say, "It does not compute." The complex intelligence of the living world is now reduced to a single binary function, and that toggle switch in the mind that can only accept a simple dualistic answer—black and white, good and evil, yes and no—is dangerously reinforced.

Our addiction to rationality has allowed us to wipe out other modes of being in the world and destroy the earth itself. In *Woman and Nature,* poet Susan Griffin describes the things that logic kills. She parodies the voice of our rational culture, a voice that speaks in absolutes. "It is decided that . . . It was discovered . . . It has been determined . . ." With reason, there is never any argument. Long ago "it was decided" that nature is an unpredictable and contentious thing, and it was left to women and to children and kept the stuff of fairy tales. In her introduction, Griffin writes,

> He says that woman speaks with nature. That she
> hears voices from under the earth. That wind blows
> in her ears and trees whisper to her. That the dead

sing through her mouth and the cries of infants are
clear to her. But for him this dialogue is over. He
says he is not part of this world, that he was set
[here] as a stranger.

And so it is Goldilocks who goes to the home of
the three bears. Little Red Riding Hood who con-
verses with the wolf, Dorothy who befriends the
lion. Snow White who talks to the birds, Cinderella
with mice as her allies, the Mermaid who is half
fish, Thumbelina courted by a mole. And when we
hear [in the Navaho chant] that a grown man sits
and smokes with bears and follows directions given
to him by squirrels, we are surprised. We had
thought only little girls spoke with animals.

Griffin has identified this antinature voice as masculine because it is a product of a predominately masculine culture. The
sad truth is that this voice exists in all of us. I do violence to
nature when I listen only to my intellect, when I abandon feeling and turn my back on what is personal and unique. Nature
is a grand undifferentiated force, and yet it demands a highly
individual response; we must know how we stand with it, and
to do that we must understand our individual weaknesses and
strengths. The Native American vision quest is an example of
this intensely personal experience; it is an exercise that allows
the initiate to confront the overwhelming forces of the natural
world. Coming to terms with that is a dangerous and demanding exercise; yet today's children do not have such an initiation.
Instead, they learn a form of abdication and begin to turn their
backs on life.

Primitive tribes used to sing the sun up and call the world to
consciousness. They had a sense that things would not be right
if they did not engage the forces of nature; without their par-
ticipation, the earth would not continue on its daily course. I
believe that we still bear the responsibility of bringing forth the
world. Yet we have so little concern for nature in our own
traditions. Our time in the garden is swiftly over, and every-

thing "important" happens after that. In Christian theology, there is no redemption of the *here and now*, no way of honoring *what is*.

We are told that humans have *dominion over* the earth, yet this belief that we are in control of things has led to an inflation that is severely damaging. It is no longer enough to be in and of the world; everything now must have a human function. To our way of thinking, if an object cannot be sold or marketed, it may be carelessly destroyed. This disregard for the sacredness of life was decried by William Wordsworth, "Getting and spending, we lay waste our powers / Little we see in Nature that is ours / We have given our hearts away."

Now, more than ever, we must try to resurrect the voices in our own tradition that speak to us about the renewal of the earth. I was grateful to discover the writings of Hildegard of Bingen, a fourteenth-century abbess who was also a spiritual guide, artist, composer, and master herbalist. Hildegard lived in the lush valley of the Rhineland, and her poems and letters are filled with the metaphors of nature. She celebrates the greenness of the soul and likens its growth to the transformation of the land. "The earth is the mother of all that is natural, of all that is human," she writes. I cannot help but wonder what Christianity would be like today if it made room for this extraordinary insight.

I have also found a welcome companion to Hildegard in the French priest and paleontologist Teilhard de Chardin. Teilhard was a theologian of a different cast, a man who believed thought was joined with eros and felt that divinity was at work within the body of the world. In *Hymn of the Universe*, he asks us to be aware of our responsibility to the earth. The world has given birth to us, and now it is the world we must redeem:

> [Children] of earth, steep yourself in the sea of matter, bathe in its fiery waters, for it is the source of your life and your youthfulness. . . .
>
> Never say, "Matter is accursed, matter is evil."

[Children] of man, bathe yourself in the ocean of matter; plunge into it where it is deepest and most violent; struggle in its currents and drink of its waters. For it cradled you long ago in your preconscious existence; and it is that ocean that will raise you up to God.

You who have grasped that the world has, even more than individuals, a soul to be redeemed, lay your whole being wide open and receive the spirit of the earth which is to be saved.

These two visionaries have come to the same conclusion as the Native American: We must protect this place, and the planet, too, must be nurtured and received.

After reading Hildegard and Teilhard, I realized that quite unconsciously I had begun to say the Lord's Prayer differently. This time it had a subtext, a kind of prayer within the prayer made room for missing elements of the feminine and nature:

Our Father who art in Heaven
Our Mother in the Earth
Hallowed be thy name
Holy be thy presence
Thy kingdom come, thy will be done
Protect this world and the life within us
on earth as it is in heaven
As we celebrate the body and the soul
Give us this day our daily bread
We give thanks for the land that nurtures us
And forgive us our debts as we forgive our debtors
Help us to love the darkness in the world and in
ourselves
Lead us not into temptation, but deliver us from evil
May our experience be whole
For thine is the kingdom and the power and the
glory forever
For yours is the wisdom of the womb and the great
round of recurring seasons
Amen.

This prayer allows me to integrate my own spiritual heritage with the things I have learned from observing nature. The words of the subtext change from one saying to the next, yet it somehow seems appropriate for the feminine lines to be responsive and to reflect our evolving portrait of the earth. This daily meditation then becomes a dialogue with life, a way of getting centered in the body of the world.

Waking Up to Nature Within

What is this great mother earth dreaming as she turns slowly in her slumber? Will her great back be broken if we do not awaken with her?

—Agnes Whistling Elk
Speaking in *Flight of the Seventh Moon*

S OME YEARS AGO I HAD A DREAM: I WAS CRADLED IN the branches of a tree in the middle of a pitch-dark forest. Rain whipped at the leaves, and the branches swayed fiercely in a strong wind. I could not open my eyes, but I felt the raging storm inside me. When I awoke, I had the strange sense that there were, in fact, no boundaries; that nature exists within us as well as without; that in the inner life of the imagination we are destined to confront the beauty and the terror of the living world.

It is curious how nightmares seduce us with their extraordinary beauty. In the dream world, we encounter the most fearful images—of fires, tidal waves, and hostile animals—and we are mesmerized. There is something hypnotic about this, and we find a certain pleasure in it. I don't believe this fascination stems from a perversity in our nature; instead, we are drawn to these images because they serve as an initiation into the mysteries of life. They affirm our suspicion that our existence cannot be completely ordered and controlled, that to learn anything new about ourselves or the universe we must surrender to the unpredictable and unknown.

The dream is nature's way of telling us how we are coping, for better or for ill, with our own drives and energies. When I was a child, I had a particularly disturbing dream: I was lying in the meadow behind our house on a moonlit night. A white wolf came through the trees and stood directly over me. I tried to call for help, but I could not make a sound. When the wolf opened its jaws, I discovered that it had no teeth. A thick, canvas-like piece of skin was stretched across its throat. This powerful creature was mute and helpless, and from this time, I began to doubt my ability to protect myself with my own voice. The wolf mirrored my own defenselessness and vulnerability, and it showed me that I was losing touch with my survival instincts. When an animal is wounded in our dreams, it is always an indication that we are about to lose something valuable in ourselves.

I have also gained important information from the *places* I inhabit in these nightly imaginings. All dreams begin by anchoring us in a given setting: *I am in an open field, and a strange man is walking toward me. I am swimming in the ocean and riding the white-crested waves. I am in a car, driving through a dark part of the city, and I am afraid.*

These opening scenes reflect a sense of being at one with the world or in conflict with my surroundings. In his *Dictionary of Symbols,* Cirlot gives the following advice: It is important to note "the shape of the terrain, whether it is undulating or broken, steeply sloped or flat, soft or hard; the relationship of the region to the surrounding area—whether it is lower or higher, more open or more enclosed; and finally the natural and artificial elements which make up the organized pattern: trees, shrubs, plants, lakes, springs, wells, rocks, sandy shores, houses, steps, benches, grottoes, gardens, fences, doors and gates." I have learned to take my cues from these inner landscapes and to ask, What places do I find threatening? Where do I feel safe?

When I dream of highways or tall buildings, for example, I know something is wrong with the pacing of my life. I am either going too fast or I am living at the "heights" and am about to lose control of things. Other times, my dream landscapes have been extremely comforting. After finishing a demanding project, I dreamed that I was staying for a time in a cottage, surrounded by ponds and flowering trees. The groundskeeper said I could stay as long as necessary to restore myself. When I asked what this place was, he told me, "You are in Verdure."

Most dreams give us information that is this personal and immediate. Every once in a while, however, we are given a "big dream" that speaks about the creation of the world. These are dreams of dinosaurs and vast, inhabited landscapes that take us back to a time when human consciousness lay dormant, a mere potential in the molten core of matter. The naturalist Annie Dillard believes that some part of the human psyche contains the land dreaming of itself, in a time long before our race was born:

> When everything else has gone from my brain—the
> President's name, the state capitals, the neighbor-
> hood where I lived, and then my own name and
> what it was on earth I sought, and then the faces of
> my friends, and finally the faces of my family—
> when all this has dissolved what will be left . . . is
> the dreaming memory of the land as it lay this way
> and that.

The earth's intelligence is articulated in and through us, and we are part of the world-dream that guides all other living things. The Australian aborigines say that nature and humans were created in "the Dream Time." They draw elaborate maps of this world, showing the moment all things came into being. Tribal healers from many different cultures go into a dream state to ask the animals and the earth to help them cure the sick (see figures 4 and 5). Like these early people, I have come to feel that dreams are nature's way of shaping our imagination and our destiny.

C. G. Jung knew that plants, animals, and the weather reflect the moods and rhythms of the human soul. Jung was aware of the continuous dialogue between the human and the earth. He felt that psyche and nature were reflections of the same reality and that a deep experience of one could be used to heal the other. For this reason, he sometimes held psychoanalytic sessions in his garden on the Lake of Zurich. In brief, he knew enough to let the psyche out of doors.

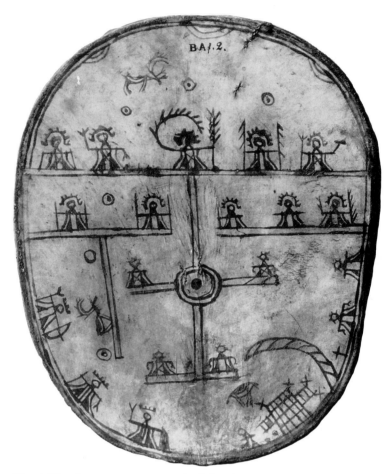

Fig. 4 *The deep, sonorous sound of the shaman's drum is designed to facilitate passage into the dream state. The drawings on the head of this drum from Lapland represent the shaman's journey to the spirit world. Here the shaman will gather dreams and visions that contribute to the wisdom of the tribe.*

Once a woman patient worried she was growing too fond of Jung and that this would be harmful to her analysis. Jung led her into his rose garden and said something to this effect: "See how the rose grows strong and healthy here? It can bloom as long as it wishes." In his inimitable way, he was also telling her, "These emotions are just a step in your own opening. You do

Fig. 5 *This shaman's mask from Ninivak Island, Greenland, depicts fish, birds, and other animals whose powers are called upon in healing rites.*

not have to be afraid of them, for eros is the true healer. You only need to cultivate this feeling that binds you to others and to the living world."

Jung knew that inner lives are grounded and supported by our contact with nature. In his autobiography, *Memories, Dreams, Reflections,* he describes the small mountain village where he lived as a boy. Here people lived close to the animals and the earth. When Jung went to the city to complete his education, however, he encountered an entirely different sensibility:

> The more I became familiar with city life, the
> stronger grew my impression that I was now getting

to know a reality that belonged to an order of
things different from the view of the world I had
grown up with in the country, among rivers and
woods, among men and animals in a small village
bathed in sunlight, with the winds and the clouds
moving over it, and encompassed by a dark night in
which uncertain things happened. It was no mere
locality on the map, but "God's world," so ordered
by Him and filled with secret meaning.

    . . . I loved all warm-blooded animals who have
souls like ourselves and with whom we have an instinctive understanding. We experience joy and sorrow, love and hate, hunger and thirst, fear and trust
in common—all the essential features of existence
with the exception of speech, sharpened consciousness and science. And although I admired science in
the conventional way, I also saw it giving rise to
alienation and aberration from God's world, as
leading to a degeneration which animals were not
capable of. Animals were dear and faithful, unchanging and trustworthy. People I now distrusted
more than ever.

The mountain people Jung was raised with were at home
with their impulses and their instincts, and they moved through
life with a certain naturalness and grace. They assumed that
everything had been done before and would be done again tomorrow; that every action, every feeling held its place in time;
indeed, that the whole of life would continue to be repeated
through the centuries with little alteration. Yet city people suffered an epidemic of self-consciousness. They were tense and
alienated from the body of the world, and this sense of dislo-
cation is even more prevalent in the present day. With our exalted egos, we no longer wish to feel that we have much in
common with the animals and the trees, and so we have removed ourselves from the larger context of creation.

In *Light Up the Cave,* the poet Denise Levertov reminds us
that only humans have abandoned the secure position enjoyed
by all other living things:

What is this joy? That no animal
falters, but knows what it must do?
That the snake has no blemish,
That the rabbit inspects his strange surroundings
in white star-silence? The llama
rests in dignity, the armadillo
has some intention to pursue in the palm-forest.
Those who were sacred have remained so,
holiness does not dissolve, it is a presence
of bronze, only the sight that saw it
faltered and turned from it.

There is a way to renew our kinship with animals and nature, and that is to go back to our first stories, to the fairy tales and legends that introduced us to the world. Children's stories are always about the animals—we begin with the owl and the pussycat and the whole menagerie that belongs to Mother Goose. We learn courage from Puss 'n Boots and compassion from Beauty and the Beast. Children identify with animals because they mirror their own instincts and energetic drives. Yet more is going on here than a mere projection of our own inner reality. We learn that the dog is not just a symbol of faithfulness— the dog actually brings this quality into our lives. When we behold any animal, we *receive* its basic nature. We partake in the fierceness of the wolf and the swiftness of the eagle. And so we must consider, when a species disappears, what capacity for human feeling also dies?

In the last generation, we have tended to dismiss both fairy tales and nursery rhymes as hopelessly naive. Yet we need to populate our stories once again with clever dogs and talking birds, with magic mice and helpful steeds. These creatures give our children a sense of agency and autonomy; they also help them to develop a belief in life.

Later on, our young people will learn very different things about their relationship to nature through scientific study. Biologists now believe that animal behavior can offer us a deeper entrée into our own evolution. In *Lives of a Cell*, for example, physician Lewis Thomas gives us an astonishing description of the traits we share with ants. "Ants are so much like human beings as to be an embarrassment," he writes. "They farm fungi, raise aphids as livestock, launch armies into wars, use chemical sprays to alarm and confuse enemies, capture slaves. . . . They exchange information ceaselessly. They do everything but watch television."

We need both kinds of stories to alert us to the humbling fact that we are not unique; indeed, we share many goals and behavior patterns with other beings. In fact, the more we are willing to give up our "superiority," the more we are able to see the richness and complexity of nature's plan.

The living world asks us to participate in its own larger story of growth and transformation. If we open ourselves to our surroundings, we are then supported as we go through our own rites of passage. A neighbor once explained that the birth of a horse played a crucial role for her in adolescence: "My best friend Sarah and I both had horses, and our whole existence was centered around these animals," she said. "When Sarah's horse foaled, it was a major event for us. She had an alcoholic father, and mine was physically violent. Things were so frightening and unpredictable. That's why this birth meant so much to us. We wanted to choose life."

Nature can put us in touch with the archetype of regeneration, and animals can even offer guidance as we go through our own turning points. By way of illustration, I would like to tell you how a deer later helped another woman through a period of transition. A few years ago, my friend was trying to leave a difficult and abusive relationship. At this time, she dreamed that a wounded doe had come to her for food and shelter. She was troubled by the dream and felt the animal had something to do with her own need to be nourished and protected. Later that week she came upon a dead fawn lying by the roadside. She carried it to a nearby field, then held a special ceremony to honor her kinship with it. As she wept for the death of this animal, she also wept for the many losses she would face. Later she explained, "Mourning the deer, I mourned the death of a two-year partnership. Yet the animal also made me think about new beginnings. I felt it had come to show me that I must always honor the preciousness of life." My friend later wrote the following poem about the ritual she improvised:

To a Fawn I Shall Bury Tonight

When Coyote danced within the sacred circle
Wind gave you legs that carried you swiftly
Earth gave you a dense coat to keep you warm
Water gave you a sharp smell to alert you
Fire gave you eyes of glowing coals.

When Coyote danced within the sacred circle
You gave us your flesh and we became strong
You gave us your coat so our feet would be warm
      walking many days.
You gave us your horns; magic for warriors
You gave us your sinew to bridle our horses.

Now Coyote does not dance within the sacred
      circle.
The sacred circle is no more.

Yet I will pick up your scattered spots
      and offer them to Father Sky.
From now on they will show the way to the true
      warrior.
And I will bury your antlers in Mother Earth
      that she may have strong medicine for
      growing trees.

To the North I offer your warm coat
To the East I offer your powerful instinct
To the South I offer your heart
To the West I offer the blood in your veins.

Until Coyote dances once more within the sacred
      circle
One of you will cease to leap
One of you will lose your thirst
One of you will sleep in the forest no more.

Our connection with the animal kingdom is both sacred and eternal. If we can remember this, we will not be alone when we experience loss or change. Instead, the whole of creation will be with us as we endure the pain of birth and transformation, and we will be comforted by the tears that are in all living things.

———————— ❀ ————————

Ritual also helps us honor our connection with nature. In earlier times, men and women found new strength in the festivals held at springtime and at harvest, and these ceremonies helped them to affirm their faith in life. In the modern era, we have made the mistake of abandoning them. We have been embarrassed by these rites because we think of them as "primitive" and "irrational," as the novelist Francine du Plessix-Gray writes in *Vogue* magazine:

> On the morning of May 1, 1949, I was the only member of the Bryn Mawr freshman class who refused to dance around the Maypole. I was up at 5 A.M. in a state of indignation, staring at the preparations of May Day with the disdain of an agnostic British colonel observing in New Delhi, some archaic ceremonial of the Indian religion. I paced my room . . . feeling proud of being an emancipated woman, some kind of a vague Marxist, a Freudian, and thus a predestined anti-Maypoler. I looked upon any ritual that savored even faintly of myth or liturgy as a vestige of humanity's childhood that must be instantly dismantled to seed the progress of mankind.

Francine du Plessix-Gray goes on to say how "the propaganda machine" of this century had prejudiced her against the dark, nonrational realm of nature and against women's rites in particular, lumping them all together with such conventions as baby showers, knitting, and garden clubs. Like many of her classmates, she wanted to excel in the male world, which had its own rituals, involving football, hunting, and military life. "The Maypole ritual bothered me then for many of the reasons I honor it now," she admits. "I see it as a profoundly female ceremony with sacred overtones, a celebration of the regeneration forces of nature, a vestige of the tree worship that has thrived in every corner of the globe. The tree was an embodiment of the Mother Goddess, a symbol of immortality and rebirth."

By the time I went to college in the 1960s, there were no rituals to rebel against. Our May Day gathering was not a rite of spring but an occasion to debate the policies of the Young Communists. Bonfires were not set to celebrate the harvest but to burn draft cards and recruitment notices. As a generation, we were well schooled in sociology and politics; we learned how people and objects work "for us" or "against us" but we did not dare to speak about the mysteries of life.

In recent years, I have turned to literature for an understanding of how things came to be this way. My first clues came from the Provençal writer Jean Giono, who wrote so eloquently about rural values. Giono says that in the nineteenth century we lost our rituals of renewal and began to make a ritual out of hoarding. The hero in *Joy of Man's Desiring* offers a solution. He urges local farmers to turn away from their obsession with accumulating and do something to restore the beauty of the world. He tells them to plant a hawthorn hedge so the wildlife can survive in winter and to use their excess grain to feed the birds. Throughout, he continually asks the people to rethink their treatment of the earth.

"I see just about what you brought here," he accuses, "goats, a cow, chicks, pigeons. Not one of you thought of bringing stags or does or nightingales or kingfishers?"

If *we* do not preserve the ark, he asks, what will become of all these creatures? And to what loathsome and impoverished state will we be reduced once the animals fail to give us joy and pleasure?

In *Song of the World*, Giono speaks about our need to open and receive the earth again. Here a blind woman describes how she feels the land inside her:

> "I know daisies, buttercups, oats, and sainfrois. They're perhaps not the same names as you give them, but that doesn't matter. It's not the names that count.
> "All the things in the world come to me in various places in my body"—she touched her thighs, her breasts, her neck, her cheeks, her forehead, and her hair—"they're tied up with me by tiny quivering strings. I myself am spring now. I am greedy like all this around us, I am full of great desires like the world."

This woman receives the revelation of the earth through her body and her senses. Giono asks us all to live from this deeper level once again, to receive our surroundings as we would the body of a lover and honor our intimacy with the mountains and the trees. Indeed, Giono would have us do the whole thing over, backing off from the technological advances that have separated us from nature. He once said of his work, "I have tried to make a story of adventure in which there should be absolutely nothing timely. I wanted new mountains, a new river, a country, forest, snow and men all new. Men who are healthy, clean and strong. They alone know the world's joy and sorrow. And this is as it should be. The others deserve neither the joy nor the sorrow. They know nothing of what they are losing. They think only of adding to their comfort, heedless that one day true men will come up from the river and down from the mountain, more implacable and bitter than the grass of the apocalypse."

This is far from a Utopian view—it is a tragic vision in which humankind is continually falling out of Paradise and losing its original contact with creation. Our hope lies in a *recorso* or a return to grace. This is only possible as long as we have access to the unspoiled hills and fields. In his novel *Harvest,* Giono tried to bring us back into our natural context—yet to portray a family at one with their surroundings he was forced to set his story in the early eighteenth century, and not in the modern world.

I have begun to think our loss of nature opens us to so many vices and addictions. When we no longer have to work to sustain the greenness of the fields, some inner voice asks if we are really needed here. We suspect that we are no longer necessary in the great scheme of creation, and so we grow compulsive in our habits and attachments; someone or something else must now provide us with that vitality and the sense of meaning that we lack. Remarkably, this idea was expressed nearly one hundred years ago, in Thomas Hardy's *Tess of the d'Urbervilles.* The Durbeyfield family is headed by a drunkard who no longer works the soil. To compensate for his own laziness, he sends his eldest daughter to work for rich relations. When the young Tess is abused by a wealthy cousin, we see how relationships disintegrate when we lose our connection with the land.

As the novel opens, Tess is dancing with the village women on the first of May to celebrate the greening of the earth. The Ladies Club of Marlot continues to uphold this pagan rite even though it has been forgotten by most of the other countryfolk. In this farming village, a woman is still so identified with nature that she is like "a portion of the field." As Tess grows to womanhood, however, we begin to see the end of this entire way of being in the world.

People used to live on the same farm all their lives and pass on their knowledge of the land. Yet Tess and the other children now receive a "standard education" that prepares them to work in the world of money and machines. Hardy tells us, "Between the mother, with her fast-perishing number of superstitions, folklore, dialect and orally transmitted ballads, and the daughter, with her trained National teachings . . . there was [now] a gap of two hundred years." When young Tess is "sent out" to work, her mother advises her to use her "woman's ways," and as Tess responds this way to d'Urberville, she brings about her own demise.

After Tess is seduced by her new employer, she moves to a neighboring county and finds work as a dairymaid. Once again she is in the lap of nature; the dairy is a place of bounty and abundance with its store of creamy butter, clotted cheeses, and the warm milk of the cows. Here Tess falls in love with Angel Clare, who has left the academic life to learn the skills of farming. We are told that he has broken away from old associations and "made close acquaintance with the seasons in their moods, the winds in their different tempers, the trees, waters and mists, shades and silences, and the voice of inanimate things."

Clare is a man in the process of discovering the beauty of the world. He watches Tess walking through the fields in the early morning light, and at such times he sees her, not as a milkmaid, but as "a visionary essence of woman—a whole sex condensed into one typical form." He calls her Artemis and Demeter and other fancy names. For a while Tess is the "earth goddess" that he seeks. When she tells him of her past, however, he abandons her and we see that he has a purely sentimental view of things. Clare does not really understand the harsh and brutal laws of nature or the down-to-earth realities of a woman's life.

This is the state of the feminine in industrial society. First a woman is taken from the land with which she feels a natural kinship, then from the protection of her family; she is looked at as an object to amuse the leisure class. She is asked to conform to the rules of male society in her role as wife, mistress, servant, or common laborer. She is not allowed to exist as a creature in and of herself. This is what happens to Tess. In the end, she is strapped to a machine, dehumanized, and cut off from the energies of life.

When Clare leaves her, Tess ends up working for her keep on some starve-acre farm. From now on, there will be no dancing in the fields. Instead, she will stoop to feed the wheat-rick, a red tyrant with straps and wheels that keeps up a despotic demand upon her muscles and her nerves. Hardy describes the demonic man who runs this machine and changes the very nature of the rural world:

> By the engine stood a dark motionless being, in a sort of trance, with a heap of coals by his side. It was the engine-man. The isolation of his manner and colour lent him the appearance of a creature . . . who had strayed into the pellucide smokeless-ness of this region of yellow grain and pale soil, with which he had nothing in common, to amaze and to discompose its aborigines.
>
> What he looked, he felt. He was in the agricultural world, but not of it. He served fire and smoke: these denizens of the field served vegetation, weather, frost, and sun. He travelled with his engine from farm to farm, from county to county, for as yet the steam-threshing machine was itinerant in this part of Wessex. He spoke in a strange northern accent; his thought being turned inwards upon himself, his eye on his iron charge, hardly perceiving the scenes around him and caring for them not at all; holding only strictly necessary intercourse with the natives as if some ancient doom compelled him to wander here against his will in the service of his Plutonic master.

Tess is placed upon the platform of this machine because her labor is the cheapest. Her body is assaulted by incessant smoke and clatter, yet she accepts this punishment without complaint. By now she has learned how to numb her spirit and her senses. As Hardy tells us, "Sheer experience taught her that in some circumstances, there was one thing better than to lead a *good* life and that was to be saved from leading any life at all."

Our very being is tied to the land and to the seasons. Yet when our culture fails to honor this—and tries to monetize all aspects of our labor—it destroys our love for the earth and for each another. Hardy has been called the most accomplished portrayer of women in English literature since Shakespeare, yet he is also a lover of the earth who cherishes its darkness and its brooding power. In his novels, he protests the nineteenth-century notion that the land and the feminine exist only as a measure of man's dominance, and in the following poem, he decries the "God of progress" who cares so little for our pleasure in this life:

> Let me enjoy the earth no less
> Because the all-enacting Might
> That fashioned forth its loveliness
> Had other aims than my delight.

In the last two hundred years, we have lost touch with our most important rituals. Our institutions and professions now fail to honor the feminine and the earth. Our lives have grown mechanical and routine. We inquire about the profits of a venture but not about its moral aims. We act for personal gain but do not stop to consider how we might harm all other living things. In *Anna Karenina,* Leo Tolstoy shows us the damage that is done by an unfeeling bureaucracy. As the story opens, we meet Count Oblonsky, a well-intentioned civil servant, and Dolly, his despairing wife. Dolly is a faithful companion who keeps both the children and the home in order. As she ages, however, her husband begins to amuse himself with other women. Oblonsky plans to sell a virgin forest to a speculator to support his current mistress. For him, the land has no intrinsic value, and he cares as little about the forest as he does about the feelings of his wife.

Dolly suffers silently to keep her family intact. Yet her sister-in-law, Anna, is a different kind of woman. She is a force of nature; her emotions are boundless and uncontained. Anna refuses to be trapped in a lifeless marriage. She leaves her husband and moves in with her lover, Vronsky. In the end, however, she pays a heavy price. Vronsky's life goes on as before: he pursues his interest in politics and attends all the important social functions while Anna loses her son and is shunned by her friends in Petersburg. In a moment of despair, she throws herself beneath a passing train.

On the day of her suicide, she dreams of a peasant working at a forge. This odious little man is a composite of the greed and indifference that permeate all levels of society.

> In early morning [she had] a terrible nightmare. . . .
> An old peasant with a tousled beard, muttering
> some meaningless French words, was doing some-
> thing as he bent over a piece of iron, while she, as
> always in this nightmare—which made it so horri-
> ble—felt that the little peasant was paying no atten-
> tion to her but was doing something dreadful over
> her with the iron. And she awoke in a cold sweat.

The peasant is so occupied with his labor that Anna's panic is ignored. There is only the constant pounding on the anvil, the incessant motion of the hammer and hand. This impenetrable man goes about his work, so devoid of feeling that he does not even notice he is about to destroy a human being.

Anna is killed by a world grown as cold and impersonal as the machine. Even her lover Vronsky behaves this way. He is so concerned with profit and efficiency that he overworks the land. Vronsky ruins the soil with modern farming methods and shows no concern for the peasants who have to make their living from these barren fields. He cares even less for animals, and when he challenges a fellow cavalry officer to a race, he cruelly mistreats his horse.

Vronsky is in the lead until he comes to a difficult water jump. The mare increases her speed, and begins to draw on her last reserves of energy. Yet Vronsky makes a rash move and then drops down into the saddle with his full weight. Her back is broken, and she struggles in the mud:

> [Vronsky] had scarely time to free his leg before Frou-Frou fell on one side; gasping painfully and making vain efforts with her delicate, sweat-covered neck to rise, she began quivering on the ground at his feet, like a wounded bird. . . .
>
> Still not understanding what had happened, Vronsky began pulling the mare by the reins. The mare again began to struggle like a fish, creaking with the flaps of the saddle, and got her front legs free, but unable to lift her hindquarters, at once began to struggle and again fell on her side. His face distorted with passion, pale, and with his lower jaw trembling, he kicked her in the belly and once more began pulling at the reins.

In the wounding of the horse, we see the wounding of the feminine and of the natural world. Vronsky fails to take responsibility for his actions. He turns his back upon the struggling mare, and later deserts Anna, refusing to confront her loneliness and isolation. Though Vronsky is admired by his peers as the perfect gentleman, his masculinity is terribly deficient. He does not know how to honor women or protect the source of life.

After reading Tolstoy, I began to wonder how men and women might relate to one another through the connecting medium of the land. I came across this invocation to an *esbat,* or holy day, recounted in *The Holy Book of Women's Mysteries* by Zsuzsanna Budapest.

I am the beauty of the green earth,
I am the white moon among the stars
The mystery of the deep waters
the desire of the human heart
Know the Mystery, therefore
Lo, I have been with you from the beginning
I am whom ye will find
at the end of your desire.

This ritual goes back some four thousand years to the sacred marriage rites of the Middle East. Here men and women lie down in the fields to celebrate the renewal of the land.

African cultures also feel this erotic bond with nature. In *The Good Life*, the geographer Yi-Fu Tuan describes the customs of the Mbuti, Pygmies of the Congo. These people make love to the forest and view all living creatures as part of their extended family:

> To the Mbuti the rain forest is protector and life-giver. They sometimes call it "Father," and sometimes "Mother." They live confidently in the midst of an all-nurturing power, to which they become emotionally attached through symbolic rites such as bathing infants in water mixed with the juice of the forest vine. An idyllic moment in their lives comes when they make love in the forest under moonlight, or when they dance alone with gestures that suggest the dancer is courting the forest.

I do not wish to revive the ideal of the noble savage. I do wish to ask, Why have we have moved so far away from our love affair with nature? And is there any way we can open up the courtship once again?

It is not too late to recast our story and put back the missing elements. Indeed, this is the challenge taken up by the French writer Michel Tournier in his novel *Friday*. Here we have a new view of Robinson Crusoe, the shipwrecked Englishman who

tries to "civilize" an island paradise. This time, our hero is not
the determined Crusoe but the manservant, Friday, the native
who knows the secrets of the earth. In Tournier's version, we
see Crusoe's flaws and character deficiencies. The Englishman
sails for the New World looking for a land to conquer, and he
does not care that he has left behind a family and a wife. This
Crusoe is not a man of feeling but a man of reason, and we see
how he uses his intellect to set himself apart from life.

In the opening scene, Crusoe scoffs at the captain's warning
that the elements of nature cannot be bent to human will. Even
when the ship is broken by a storm and he is washed up on a
deserted shore, he stubbornly insists upon his own supremacy.
Crusoe declares himself the ruler of this lonely place and dubs
himself "the Governor of Speranza." He makes a plow, designs
an irrigation system, and even puts a porch on the makeshift
cottage he grandly calls "The Residence." Yet the island fails
to yield to him; it has a will of its own, a power and a presence
he cannot begin to tame.

One day Crusoe discovers a glade on the far side of the island. This is Friday's hiding place and the only piece of earth
that Crusoe has not tried to change. When he is alone in this
virgin place, something new begins to happen. Crusoe lies down
on the soft wet earth and begins to make love to it. Tournier
describes this union in one of the most sensuous passages in all
of modern literature:

> He felt as never before that he was lying on Speran-
> za as if on a living being, that the island's body was
> beneath him. Never before had he felt this with so
> much intensity, even when he walked barefoot
> along the shore that was teeming with so much life.
> The almost carnal pressure of the island against his
> flesh warmed and excited him. She was naked, this
> earth that enveloped him, and he stripped off his
> own clothes. Lying with arms outstretched, his loins
> in turmoil, he embraced that great body scorched
> all day by the sun, which now exuded a musky

sweat in the cooler air of the evening. He buried his face in the grass roots, breathing open-mouthed, a long, hot breath. And the earth responded, filling his nostrils with the heavy scent of dead grass and the ripening of seeds, and of sap rising in new shoots. How closely and how wisely were life and death intermingled at this elemental level! His sex burrowed like a plowshare into the earth, and over-flowed in immense compassion for all created things. A strange wedlock, consummated in the vast solitude of the Pacific! He lay exhausted, *the man who had married the earth.* . . . [emphasis mine]

When Crusoe looks down on the gentle, rolling meadow, he sees a covering of pink-tinted grass, like a coat of hair. "It's a coomb," he murmurs to himself, "a pink coomb." This is an old English word for valley or dale—but Crusoe thinks of a comb and hair flowing down the back of a naked woman. For him, the land has taken on the appearance of the beloved. He rests his hand on a mound of earth, as he would upon a woman's breast.

Crusoe now knows why Friday comes to this secluded mound. He is also dimly aware that this mating with the earth recalls some ancient ritual. The word *coomb* has a meaning that he can't quite remember. It is linked to the Celtic goddess Cunna, who was known as the mother of creation and the moving force in all relationship.

This novel shows us that it is virtually impossible to abandon nature, for no matter how obstinately "civilized" we become, it is still alive within us. It may take us some time to discover it, yet the earth is always trying to redeem us, to bring us back to her through our imagination and our senses. Our dreams and erotic longings, then, may be the truest instruments of evolution, for they wed us to the passion of the living world.

We don't need to travel to an island paradise to have this experience. Our dreams and mating rituals remind us that we are still a part of nature. Yet, like Crusoe, we must give up our desire to control our surroundings and learn how to receive the living world. I have come to believe that nature moves within us like the unseen forms that shift and breathe beneath the continents. Often, we do not take the trouble to find out what goes on in this deeper place. If we pay attention, we will find that something different is required of us. Life asks us to open and surrender to it. We are only vessels or containers, not the masters that we seem.

Bringing Back the Feminine

No woman should be shamefaced when attempting, through her work, to give back to the world a portion of its lost heart.

—Louise Bogan

I AM AN ANIMIST: I BELIEVE THAT EVERYTHING IS LIVING, even this machine, and that my computer receives my thoughts the way an old pair of shoes receives the spirit of its owner. I have always refused to think of matter as a dead coordinate, a fixed butterfly pinned to a canvas without movement, without life. Who says it's naive to feel connected to the physical world, to remember that the entire galaxy was spewed forth from the same parentage and so we are related to the planets and the stars? And what's so odd, as Annie Dillard says, about teaching a stone to talk? This is a wonderful reversal for it shows that, after centuries of trying to master nature, we are the ones who must learn to do the listening and resonate with all creation once again.

This is the gift of the feminine—it is quite simply our way of receiving the beauty of the world. At its most developed, the feminine principle maintains a profound respect for nature and a deep empathy for all other living things. Yet it is difficult to achieve this view in a society that runs on logic and analysis. We are very far from the feminine, indeed, when we fail to identify with matter. Reason then takes precedence over feeling, ideas are disembodied, and we destroy our capacity for relatedness.

This bias has been built into our present institutions, and we learn to turn our backs on the feminine at a very early age. As soon as children enter grammar school, they are removed from the body of the mother and from the body of the earth. Historian Marilyn Chapin Massey points out that kindergarten originated in nineteenth-century Germany to provide an introduction to the Fatherland and to teach a masculine way of ordering the world. Educators argued that a woman could not be trusted with her children because she might turn them over to a wet nurse who was "morally degenerate" or fill their heads with fantasies and fail to keep the proper discipline. To the rational mind, the feminine was considered disruptive and even dangerous. Woe to the mother who allowed her children to follow their own instincts! No little Emile, no child of nature, had a place in this new hierarchy. That is because the nineteenth century had no faith in nature or in the content of a woman's soul.

Theologians even questioned whether women could be sufficiently separated from their own nature to become the proper instruments of a Christian education. Ministers liked to tell the story of "good Gertrude," an obedient wife who obeyed the wishes of her husband "more qualified" to raise a child. One reformer was so disappointed in women and in their inability to be "good Gertrudes" that he lamented, "The mothers of this land will not do it! . . . as Christ once cried out to Jerusalem, 'Mothers! Mothers! we would have gathered you together under the wings of wisdom, humanity, and Christianity, as a hen gathereth her chickens, *But ye would not.*'"

The nineteenth century proposed an ideal of divine motherhood suitably removed from all dirty things like matter, instinct, and the earth itself. And so it conjured up a contradictory image of the feminine: a "mother hen with chicks"—who would willingly forego the promptings of the natural world!

Today we are struggling to bring education back to the experiential, to involve the emotions and the senses and reinstate those feminine values the previous century so vehemently rejected. In *The Magical Child,* Joseph Chilton Pearce observes that imagination and feeling develop at ages five through seven, and this is the time when children need to indulge in fantasy and storytelling for their own development. Unfortunately, we have begun to teach the abstract rules of logic and arithmetic at this tender age. Chilton Pearce says that this training goes against the grain of childhood and removes the mind from its true context.

Educators are under pressure from many quarters, however, to put forth highly conceptual views. In 1988, a group of eminent scientists expressed their dismay that most young children think the earth is flat. The scientists blamed this on current teaching methods, yet I believe that these children have an age-appropriate picture of the world. They are at that stage of life where the wisdom of their senses naturally predominates. The earth is flat because that's how it *appears to be*. It is wrong to insist that they accept on faith a "scientific" system that has no basis in their immediate reality. The concept of gravity and the curvature of the earth belong to a later developmental state, and in insisting on this scientific "truth," we teach children to blindly follow doctrine and distrust their own experience.

In earlier times, education began with the unity of mind and nature. Yet in the modern era, we have had the nature all washed out of us. We have been taken from the body of our mothers and plucked from the body of the earth and forbidden to explore the mind we share with all creation. Education has now degenerated into mere instruction, providing us with a series of operational directions, a basic manual of "How Things Work." I recall my own frustration, sitting as though imprisoned in a classroom, waiting for ideas to take root, without honoring the body and the emotions as their germinating ground. To understand a thing, we must first feel drawn to it. Our longing for the world is what inspires us. It is like air and sunlight to an unfolding flower. Without it, we are kept from our own opening and from a direct experience of life.

It was not until college, when I began to study early Greek philosophy, that I found any support for my love of nature and my emerging concept of the feminine. From the start, I was attracted to the Pre-Socratics who often wrote as poets about the glories of the universe. Heraclitus said, "All things are full of souls and spirits"; Thales, that the "soul is intermingled" with matter; Anaximenes, that we must revere the breath for it connects us to the respiration of the cosmos; Anaximander, that the earth is constantly creative and that its many life forms are always *in relationship.*

The Greeks believed that the earth was our primary teacher and spoke of "a great vibrant being, a living breathing body, a heart, a spirit, a soul, a goddess." It was a feminine entity called Gaea, and she was the creator of creators. This goddess was embodied in our language in the words genesis, genus, genitals, genetics, and generation.

When I began this course I felt I understood these early philosophers in my own way. I had treasured memories of my grove of trees, and that period in my youth when I felt mothered by the land. Imagine my dismay when this tradition was soundly ridiculed. These writers were not empiricists, I was informed, and so I could not take them seriously. Logic was the only thing of interest; we had to see the mind at work and deny this more poetic vision. Yet I was not sure exactly why we had to choose: Couldn't intellect make room for feeling and for intuition? Why was there only one way to probe the mysteries of the living world?

By the time I worked my way up to the moderns, I had experienced a great deal of discomfort. In "The Republic," Plato espoused equal education for women, but from then on I faced a full-scale rejection of the feminine and the earth. Aristotle considered both women and nature his inferiors. Aquinas said anything feminine was "derived"; Bacon, that love and marriage were serious "impediments"; Hobbes, that the world was hostile and life in a state of nature was "nasty, brutish, and short."

I felt a momentary reprieve, however, as we moved into the eighteenth century to study Leibniz and his best-known work, *The Monadology.* Much to my surprise, I found the same reverence for the living world that was so attractive in the ancient

Greeks. Leibniz said that the whole of life was reflected in the smallest unit of reality. "The monad is the many contained in the one," he wrote. "[It is] a full articulation of the universe. . . ." Here I did not have to choose between mind and matter; instead, I saw the soul at work within the body of creation.

Leibniz was a cosmologist—and also something of a mystic—yet to my astonishment, he was taught as a *logician* complete with rules and syllogisms. This was the opinion of our instructor, a neurasthenic little man who seemed to thrive in the narrow capillaries of thought and to sustain himself in these nether regions without the benefit of light or air. His bias kept us from the most important discovery of all—that the monad, in its extraordinary richness and complexity, was nothing less than the intelligence of the living universe.

By now, a philosopher seemed to me a rational man removed from the body and the senses, a solitary ruminator who railed against the trials of the ordinary world. I was amused to find that in Louisa May Alcott's view, a philosopher was like "a man up in a balloon with his family and friends holding the ropes which confine him to the earth and trying to haul him down." I wondered if this was the duty of the feminine—to simply keep the thinkers on the ground.

My humor enabled me to get through most of the semester. Yet at one point, things began to take a much more serious turn. In my final essay for philosophy, I mourned our increasing loss of nature and asked, "If this is the price for progress, why is no one speaking from the heart?" My effort was rejected because I had not spent enough time discussing Locke and the English social contract. This refusal of my paper echoed the wound that I had suffered in many areas of my life: the sense that the feminine didn't really count, that feelings were unimportant, and that we could exist without the deep, abiding comforts of the earth. At the end of the year, I checked into the Lahey Clinic and discovered a massive tumor on my ovary. Two days later, I gave birth to five pounds of rejected tissue because

I had not been allowed to give birth to the feminine in my writing and my work.

Our academic disciplines have steadily retreated from the natural world, so our dialogue is distorted; when vital energies appear, they may come through as illnesses and as aberrations. As the psychologist Robert Sardello said at the Dallas Institute of the Humanities: "The abstract world needs flesh. . . . A body is trying to materialize in cancer, for that is what the world is in need of." It took me many years to see how my tumor was related to my disembodied education. Yet now I see how all of us are wounded when we train the mind to work without the senses and the brain to labor on without the subtle wisdom of the heart.

I have since learned two ways to heal ourselves and restore our contact with the feminine—one is to get our hands into the earth, and the other is to dig around in the loamy soil of the unconscious and begin to pay attention to our dreams. Dreams reveal the ideas that are trying to take root in the human soul; they are clues to the attitudes we need to bring about our own renewal and to the kind of inner work we must do to achieve a more balanced way of life.

While I was still an undergraduate, I began to have a series of dreams about the sheer inadequacy of my formal education and its rejection of the feminine. In the first one, I conjured up my old professor; I called him up to tell him that I understood the monadology, but this time, I would have to explain it in my own terms. To my surprise, he would not even speak to me. Instead, he sent a small boy to meet me in a shopping mall. The boy was a hostile little urchin who stole my purse and dumped out its contents. I was left stooping down to retrieve my feminine possessions, feeling embarrassed and humiliated. This dream showed me that I was still at war with the masculine and with the basic teachings of Western philosophy.

Some years later, I began to write a thesis on Virginia Woolf and the new feminine psychology. As I approached the end of my research, I had a terrifying dream: I had discovered the female equivalent of the Oedipal complex—yet the penalty for this was death! I began to despair that the kind of knowledge I longed for was "forbidden" by our culture and that I would need more courage than I suspected to unearth my feminine authority.

To enter this new mode, I would have to put aside my academic training and stop deferring to the experts. I could no longer rely upon "the standard sources," whether I was quoting Melanie Klein and Karen Horney or Dewey, Freud, and Jung. For a long time I had been so unsure of my perceptions that I hid behind the words and thoughts of others. At this point, I dreamed that I was lecturing at a university on a new theory of social revolution. An aggressive and intelligent woman stepped forward and asked me where I got that notion. I was afraid to say, "From my own experience," and so I replied, "From C. G. Jung. I always attribute anything worthwhile to him." It was clear that the rules must be changed: I now had to trust my own experience and remember that the main text was my life.

Why, I wondered, is it so hard for women to live according to their own inner nature—to stand behind their values and their feelings? The poet Muriel Rukeyser once said the world would split open if women dared to openly speak their truth. Perhaps our most urgent need is not to shatter worlds but to *re-create* them. I thought about a new form of education that would restore us to the body and the senses, as I began to dream about a different kind of school:

> I am driving down a wide street in Manhattan, looking for my school. I park in a deserted area of town and keep walking until I hear voices.
>
> Suddenly I am on a wooden bridge, crossing over a stream. There are bushes, rocks, and trees, and I am in a rural landscape. At the end of the path, I find a modest house.
>
> I enter and begin to set the table for a family. I put out delicate homemade cookies called "ladyfingers"—one plate for the children and another for

adults. The woman comes in from the yard, her
hands the color of earth. Her husband arrives and
then the children. I am going to eat with them and
live here for a while. I realize this is my school!

I did not take the dream literally and immerse myself in cook-
ing and in domestic chores; instead, I knew that I was being
called upon to find new life in my relationships, to come
"home" to my own vision of the feminine.

In the last few years, many of my friends have experienced a
similar need to "regrow" themselves as women, and in the process, we have discussed our common images and themes. This
reschooling of the feminine is primary among them. A friend
who is also a psychotherapist has written, "Our challenge is to
move from Alma Mater to Mater Natura, to undergo a process
of re-education that will reconnect us to the core of life." At
forty, this woman also began to sense the incompleteness of her
college training. She recorded what she called her "Back to
Vassar" dreams, which helped restore the values that were missing from her youthful education. In the final dream, she returned to Vassar and found no buildings, only the ground on
which the college stood:

> I walk down a narrow path through the pines and
> come to a big round domed building, grey and over-
> grown. It is "Esse House." I find a Latin grammar
> book with a mystical feeling about it which tells me
> that in Latin *esse* means *to be*.
>
> I return to the original path and keep walking, til
> I come to an overlook where a young man and
> young woman are leaning on a rustic wooden rail
> and gazing at the view. I look and am amazed to
> see a wonderful view of the Hudson River, with lit-
> tle houses in the hills just like the paintings of the
> river from the early nineteenth century. We couldn't
> see the Hudson from the campus before. It is so
> much more beautiful than I remembered it, that I
> begin to weep. I am overwhelmed by the loveliness

of nature and the snowy, pinegreen freshness of the
campus now.

My friend later wrote about this dream: "I was on the land
long before it was the host to Vassar. 'Esse House' is a temple
to the feminine mode of being that was hidden during my college days. In this place, I learn that it is the nature of woman
to abide and to ground herself in the essence of life. In the
dream there is very little thinking going on; I simply walk along
a path, looking at what I see, enthralled by being at one with
the beauty of the land."

We must all learn how to balance out our rational education
with a sense of being in and of the world. To do so we must
ask, What is this knowledge *for?* And how does it *serve the
earth?*

Education is not an end in itself but a means of reconciling
ourselves with nature and with our own *inner* environment. To
begin this process, we have to sacrifice our addiction to rationality and control and to a one-sided way of thinking. The Jungian analyst Irene Claremont de Castillejo says in *Knowing
Woman* that so far we have failed to pay attention to the direct
experience of nature that young women need: "On the one
hand, women are educated to accept man's values blindly.
Schools and colleges have ... accepted without question the
masculine over-valuation of a thinking function and of physical
prowess. Girls have adopted the ability to do mathematics as a
test of intelligence and a capacity for games as the criterion of
bodily perfection. Many an inferiority complex stems from
these mistakes." Castillejo says woman must keep in touch with
the springs of life, "with the inseparable connection of all growing things and their eternal continuity."

As I considered this alternative way of being, my own dreams
began to change. This time I dreamed about leaving the traditional male college and taking a new path that led me back to
nature. Finally I had come to understand my place within the
body of creation:

I am at an all-men's college in Connecticut. The students are all my age: thirty-five. Some men tell me they can get me office space at the college; they show me a building with two huge brass doors, yet I notice a forbidding plaque that says, "Do not enter here."

Suddenly I am alone by the sea: the moon is huge and the Milky Way is shining. I am stunned by the power and beauty of this night. The waves are being pulled higher and higher by the full moon. I am unafraid of nature because I know how to deal with this phenomenon. I know this is a Woman's storm.

The feminine is personal; once we connect with it, we can no longer judge each other by our abstract titles and achievements. We know it is wrong and somehow demeaning to reduce ourselves to job descriptions and to ignore the many other ways of being in the world. I once heard the artist Allan Gussow speak to a group of educators. He explained how the standard resume isolates the individual from ordinary life. Gussow then took time to explain just how his work fits into the rhythm of the day:

Here are some of the things I do: I paint on summer mornings before breakfast, in winter after coffee, with cedar incense and fine cigars. I read poetry, listen to Indian ragas and Charles Ives, stretch canvas and rub my fingers over raw linen. I dig in the garden, compost egg shells and orange peels, plant seeds and harvest slowly, build fences and make boundaries, watch fresh leaves lifting earth, cut grass, and walk in the yard looking at our big green Victorian house from all sides. I eat

> raw greens on all fours, nibble brussels sprouts,
> kale and stalks of asparagus, collect wild mush-
> rooms, buy books, ride a ten-speed bike, give
> speeches and organize exhibits, talk . . . and make
> love with my wife, smile with my boys, answer let-
> ters slowly, camp at least once in winter, help other
> artists to reclaim their places and remember where I
> have been . . .

This description is wonderfully appealing; it encourages us to reclaim our senses and revive our connection to the living world. It also reminds us: "Put aside your *persona* and get *personal*; drop your mask and dare to be seen for who you really are."

The feminine principle can also help us move beyond our one-dimensional view of people and of organizations. We are beginning to understand that something terrible happens both to nature and to our *human* nature when our emphasis is solely on efficiency and profit. We spend so much time "pushing numbers" that we soon grow oblivious to the feeling content of our work. The feminine tells us to address what we like and dislike about our jobs, to take note, not just of our talents and abilities, but of the state of mind they evoke.

Fifteen years ago, I worked at a large publishing company in charge of publicity and special projects; my work involved interviewing people whom I found challenging and inspiring. Yet at certain times of the year I had to sit alone in my office scrutinizing stacks of raw demographic data and illuminate that year's pattern of consumer spending. I was unaware how much I resented working with statistics until I dreamed that I was forced to speak in numbers, not in words:

> I am in midtown Manhattan, riding in a limousine
> with a businessman who is busily reading the stock
> market quotes. He tells me that X stock is selling at
> 49.7. The driver mumbles, "That's gratitude for
> you," because we do not speak to him.

> The businessman and I get out at Grand Central Station and begin running for our trains. He says that I could at least make conversation while we are running. I look at him and angrily shout, "49.7!"

The key question here is this: Who is doing the real work? The driver gets me from place to place and makes an obvious and practical contribution to my life. But I am sitting in back with the businessman whose conversation bores me. This is how I always felt when I was knee-deep in market studies. Years later I understood my resistance to this kind of task. The Jungian analyst Marie-Louise von Franz has written: "You do not realize what it does to you when you read statistics. It is a completely destructive poison and what is worse is that it is not true; it is a falsified image of reality. If we begin to think statistically, we begin to think against our own uniqueness. Probability is only one way of explaining reality and as we know, there is just as much uniqueness and irregularity. When the statistical way of thinking gets people, it always means that they have either no feeling or weak feeling, or that they tend to betray their own feeling. . . . When [we do this] we cut the soul in two" (*Puer Aeternus*). This mechanistic view is against nature and against our human nature. When faced with statistics or with a new invention, we must continually ask, Who does this serve? And what is the effect upon the human soul?

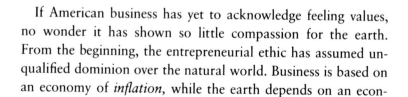

If American business has yet to acknowledge feeling values, no wonder it has shown so little compassion for the earth. From the beginning, the entrepreneurial ethic has assumed unqualified dominion over the natural world. Business is based on an economy of *inflation*, while the earth depends on an economy of *conservation*. Is there any way to reconcile these two opposing attitudes?

It might help us to go back to the beginning and look at the original connection between money and the land. In *Magic, Myth and Money,* William Desmonde reminds us that money was invented, not as a possession, but as a magic talisman. It was originally a symbol for community and for the earth's renewal. Money evolved from the practice of sharing food and goods—and this exchange was rooted in religious ritual, celebrating friendship, loyalty, and the bonds of human love. "Almost every object we can think of has in one culture or another been used as money," Desmond writes. "Whale's teeth, feathers, beads, rice, drums, gong, cannon, bee's wax, tea, salt, cocoa and reindeer."

"The cowry shell," he continues, "was employed as money in early Egypt and represented the Great Mother, creator of the human family. Thus one of the earliest forms of money indicated powers of fertility." Money was not something abstract as it is today. Instead, it was related to the powers of the feminine and to the cycles of rebirth. When a match was made, the two families exchanged their most valuable belongings. In this way, a covenant was made. It said, "I give you food and clothing, and I will also give you life."

By the Middle Ages, money had become symbolic of spiritual transformation: "In an ideal sense, the quest for money is identical with the search for the Holy Grail," Desmond suggests. "A persistent motif in the legend is a blight upon the land, resulting from the weakening vitality of the king. The knight's quest for the sacred vessel, then, is actually a type of initiation in which the seeker's task is to find the source of grace and energy lacking both within the country and within himself." The question is, can money once again become the link between nature and spirit, between the human and the earth?

I believe something of this connection still remains. The coins in our pockets are little symbols of the value of the material world. No wonder we dream of money stolen, lost, or found!

Part of the psyche remembers that money is related to the energies of life. Our first economic systems were all related to the cycles of the living world. Native Americans held giveaways on a yearly basis to keep the goods in circulation, while the Aztecs *destroyed* their economic surplus every other generation. The idea was to pave the way for regeneration and for a new phase of life. I believe we feel unconsciously compelled to sacrifice our prosperity—indeed, that may be what's behind the economic downswings and depressions that plague us roughly every fifty years.

Experts have charted a long-wave economic cycle of alternating booms and busts. They have also told us that we are virtually powerless to change the pattern of prosperity and depression. We have been through three global recessions since the 1790s, with major downturns during the Battle of Waterloo, the Civil War, and the Roaring Twenties, and another downswing is predicted in the next two years. Perhaps we should learn how to value this pattern as a natural corrective for our abuses of the earth. These may stem from a "primitive conscience" that understands that everything in life is governed by the earth's organic cycles. We may call this conscience "superstitious" and "irrational," but it appears to be intent on honoring the very real limits to growth and on maintaining our deep connection to the land. Our inability to manipulate the world through human economics, then, may be less of a shortcoming and more like a blessing in disguise.

In the long run, we must learn how to view economics from the inside out. This is the purpose of the feminine: it tells us to stop trying to impose our ideas and begin to listen to the organic nature of the thing itself. Only in this way can we bring our culture into harmony with the body of the world.

It is time to take a second look at all professions and bring them back in contact with the feminine and the earth. Business is not the only discipline that has lost touch with these basic values; we have watched them disappear from the sciences as well. Physicist Brian Swimme has said, "We give young people the skills to change the genetic code, to alter natural processes. Then we send them off to work for major companies, and at no time are they asked to question how they will use these god-like powers." His point is well taken. Our colleges have become like trade schools; we prepare a generation of technicians to manipulate the world and yet neglect to speak to them of its integrity and autonomy.

As we read the newspaper these days, we are constantly reminded that the old systems are breaking down and we need new ways—feminine ways—to view our planet. The masculine principle calls on us to take apart and analyze; its primary orientation is toward the moment of intellectual discovery and not the moment in which we encounter life. In 1988, a team of scientists went into the Alaskan wilderness in search of "Bigfoot," the legendary Sasquatch. One scientist told the Associated Press how they planned to deal with their unusual subject: "We want to kill it so we can bring it back and analyze it. Then it can be protected." This is the kind of logic that has already destroyed many other species. What's worse, this is the attitude we now plan to carry into outer space in our attempt to conquer other worlds.

That same year, the *New York Times* reported on the activities of the Princeton Space Studies Institute, a private nonprofit corporation that proposes to mine the riches of other planets and exploit their moons and asteroids. These futuristic schemes were described in the matter-of-fact way that one might talk of building a shopping center: ". . . the generally agreed-upon plan went something like this: First we go to the Moon, where, taking advantage of the low lunar gravity and resources available in space, we establish an outpost from which to launch [other] expeditions. . . . Many of the presentations were by private entrepreneurs and consultants who believe [this] can be not only adventurous but profitable. The papers were technical in nature, but they reflect a confidence that technology can render space as conquerable as any frontier."

The problem is we are just beginning to see the damage we have done to our own frontiers. We have disrupted our own ecology and wish to avoid the necessary healing and repair: Now the experts tell us all we have to do is steal our resources from other planets. Of course, this same mentality allowed nineteenth-century empires to prosper at the expense of outlying regions. In *Ideas About the Future,* Adrian Berry predicts that the buck will not stop there. Indeed, "the bloody histories of colonial conquests here on earth will probably be repeated . . . and alien communities destroyed so that adventurers from earth can fill the holds of their ships with some precious commodity."

I believe that things will not go well if we move into space to carry out a hostile process. Where is our regard for natural process? And for the spirit of these foreign worlds? Our purely commercial intent was made clear at the Princeton conference by Brian O'Leary in his paper on extracting water from Phobos and Demos, the Martian moons. "With the investment of four Mars trips over a period of eight years we have the means to deliver several thousand metric tons of water to Earth orbit, lunar orbit, and the surfaces of the Moon by 2003. More equipment could be delivered to the Moon to support a lunar base which could be supplied by Phobos-Demos water . . . [and] the space renaissance will have begun" (*New York Times,* May 24, 1988).

Will this renaissance be based on a full-scale disturbance of another planetary ecosystem? In Greek mythology, Demos and Phobos are the sons of Mars known as Fear and Terror. The ancient Celts also had a saying: "In Demos was a terrible demon born, full of fire and blood." Perhaps protest will come from the deeper structures of the cosmos, from the realm of the unpredictable and unknown.

Long ago we lost our connection with the earth's (
and, with it, our understanding of the feminine—of th
ability of nature and the earth's own cycles of death a
eration. In *Moon, Moon,* Anne Kent Rush reminds us
moon once regulated our fertility as well as the time f(‿ pıaııt-
ing and brought together the reproductive cycles of the human
and the earth. In this book, she reminds us how important it is
to approach the moon with a different kind of energy. The
political use of space flights and the aspect of claiming yet another piece of the cosmos for "mankind" annoy her. If she went
to the moon, she wouldn't have done it that way: "I certainly
wouldn't have tried to signify any territorial power . . . [or]
tried to transfer my earth consciousness to this foreign place.
Instead Rush would have tried to learn the ways of this new
environment by . . . sensing the new ecology."

She goes on to suggest we learn to balance our outward explorations with a kind of "inner knowing," and offers us a
ritual to identify with the moon and honor its role in both our
imagination and in our daily lives:

Let us paint our faces white & dance to the moon
Let us wear black robes & dance to the moon
So that we can feel the whiteness of the moon's face
And the blackness of the sky surrounding her.

We dance on the night when the moon is full
Because we know her movement in our bodies
And in the bodies of plants and of animals
And in the body of their mother the black sea.

We sing to the Moon our Sister
We sing to the Moon our Mother
We sing to the Moon, our Night Lover
And we sing for the love of each other.

The question now remains: Can we revive this feminine wisdom? Can reason serve the imagination and science begin to

know its boundaries? Can we combine these two views to produce a third, and as yet unknown, way of being in the world?

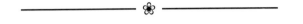

In *Notes Towards the Definition of Culture*, T. S. Eliot says that every society starts out with a unified purpose. Then the original vision wanes, and we see the rise of new elites. These subgroups can revitalize the main frame of a culture. When they succumb to vanity and competition, we have reached a danger point. How can we regain our solidarity?

First we have to move from a worldview that is *egocentric* to a worldview that is ecocentric. Most organizations are still operating in the egocentric model—and on the basis of our childish wants and needs. Yet some people are trying to define a more mature approach and to create institutions that are self-renewing and organic like the biosphere itself. In Minneapolis, business consultant Magaly Mossman asks her clients to consider the following criteria for a new venture: "Does this project draw equally on masculine and feminine values? Does it honor intuition as well as rationality? Does it involve all in the decision-making? Does it respect the earth's resources? Is it ecologically sound?"

This is innovative work, and it supports the basic values of all living systems. Yet this "organic" way of doing things is not completely new: Many of these principles can be found in older cultures that were more dependent on the land. The *I Ching*, an oracle widely used at the height of the Chou dynasty (sixth century B.C.) and still consulted in China today, advises that all institutions must be in balance with the earth. "To build a satisfactory social organization, we must go down to the very foundations of life. For any merely superficial ordering . . . that leaves the deepest needs unsatisfied, will be as ineffectual as if no attempt had been made."

It is the role of the masculine principle to help us see distinctions, to separate and clarify. The feminine role is to reconcile and unify. Today we must remember the value of the whole. Despite our varying degrees of wealth and education, we are but a single species interacting with the earth. In southern France, there is an icon of the Virgin Mary called the *Vierge Ouvrante,* literally, "the opening virgin." Inside Mary's body, we find the living world: All the animals are preserved within her womb, and her entire being is a landscape containing mountains, lakes, and trees. If we approach this image consciously, we will see that the earth is like a spiritual mother who is calling us to be a part of her larger destiny.

The planet itself does not see us as partisans, nor does it take note of our politics and ideology. Its primary goal is wholeness: to enfold our many visions into her own ecology. This is what feminine consciousness is also trying to achieve. In its most developed form, it asks us to receive "the other" and to enlarge and expand our own identity.

I believe the feminine principle is evolving at this very moment and a new and vital strength is trying to come into this world. I have seen evidence of this in my own dreams and in the dreams of others—men as well as women. The message is the same. An inner voice says, "Be patient. There is a deeper ground to your existence. You are more than a number or a fragment; remember you are the carrier of life." To refuse the feminine is to refuse the call to transformation that permeates the universe. Can we defend ourselves against this force with mere concepts and ideas? I sincerely doubt it. John Milton knew the limits of our reason when he warned, "Though all the winds of doctrine were let loose to play upon the earth . . . we do ingloriously to misdoubt her strength" (*Aereopagitica*).

TWO

Rituals of Completion

Initiation as a Gateway to the Earth

I think I am here on this earth to present a report on it, but to whom I do not know.

—Czeslaw Milosz
Unattainable Earth

WHEN I WAS TWELVE, I WOULD COME HOME FROM school and give my father an account of the day's activities. I performed this exercise, faithfully offering up my list of good deeds and accomplishments, hoping to validate my place in the world. Yet one day a dream revealed that something else existed beneath the ordered surface of my life. In the dream, my father and I were sitting in our living room when suddenly the floor began to rip and fall away beneath me. I was plummeted down a long, dark tunnel toward the center of the earth. I awoke, terrified that I had fallen into the abyss with no hope of returning. Many years later, I understood the message of this dream: We are not only responsible to people and to institutions in the world above but to the deeper values of the earth. It is not to family, friends, or community that we owe our main allegiance. Rather, it is to the life force of this planet that we must ultimately report.

The dark tunnel has long been a feature of initiation rites. In the early matriarchies, supplicants would crawl on their bellies into a cave or labyrinth and make their journey down into the center of the earth. This exercise was meant to be disorienting and frightening. The people left behind their ordinary occupations and identities and surrendered to the dark womb of creation. After a time of prayer and fasting, they emerged from this place, strengthened and reborn.

An experience of the darkness is necessary for our own transformation, and we, too, are connected to the organic cycles of the earth. Indeed, a universal pattern of death and resurrection guides our psychological development as surely as it guides the natural world. We can see this process at work in the stories of the Sumerian goddess Inanna and the Greek maiden Persephone.

Inanna goes down to the Underworld and is stripped of all her finery. As she passes through the seven gates, she relinquishes her scepter, her jewels, and her robes, until she stands naked before the Queen of Death. Once Inanna sacrifices the symbols of her wordly power, she is turned into a corpse. She hangs on the death pole for three days until the Queen of Death is finally tricked into releasing her. In the first stage of initiation, Inanna gives up her exalted place and comes to understand the dark side of the universe. In the second, she is resurrected, and her suffering brings new meaning to the world.

In the fields of Eleusis, Persephone makes a similar descent. When we first meet her, she is a young virgin wandering aimlessly through the meadow, a child-woman who has not yet awakened to the full reality of life. Then she is abducted by Hades and taken to the Underworld. While this seems a terrible thing, Persephone nevertheless finds some nourishment here. She eats four pomegranate seeds; the red, moist fruit recalls the fertile womb, and the four seeds represent the first four months of the earth's own generative cycle. Persephone remains in Hades when the land lies fallow; then she returns to her mother, the great goddess of the earth, who joyfully renews the bounty of the vineyards and the fields.

Inanna and Persephone show how abundance and fertility spring forth from darkness. The descent may begin with a death, with abduction, or abandonment. The message of feminine spirituality is unflinching: This experience of loss is a prerequisite for the growth and transformation of the world.

During the Persian Wars, some thirty thousand regularly celebrated the Persephone descent to Hades' realm and her subsequent rebirth. Philosophers, historians, and poets were among the inductees, and we find references to these ceremonies in Plato, Homer, and Herodotus. While the populace gathered once a year to reenact these mysteries, Attic priests routinely descended into a ceremonial pit (abaton) to renew their contact with the living earth. As Barbara Walker writes in *The Woman's Encyclopedia of Myths and Secrets,* it was thought that this would help them develop their prophetic powers.

> The abaton was standard equipment in a pagan temple. Those who entered it to incubate, or to sleep overnight in magical imitation of the incubation in the womb, were thought to be visited by a spirit who brought prophetic dreams. Novice priests went down into the pit for longer periods of incubation, pantomiming death, burial, and rebirth from the womb of Mother Earth. Once initiated in this way, they were thought to gain the skill of oneiromancy: the ability to interpret dreams.
>
> The same burial and resurrection ritual is found in the lives of many ancient sages. It was said that Thales of Miletus, accounted one of the Seven Wise Men of the ancient world, . . . derived his intellectual skills from communion with the Goddess of Wisdom in an abaton.

The labyrinth or passageway cut deep into the earth was a familiar symbol in the ancient world. It was inscribed on coins and at the entrance to ceremonial caves and tombs. The Cretan king Minos constructed a labyrinth beneath the palace at Knossos; Minos was known as the Lord of Death, and his labyrinth was patterned on the River Styx, which wove in and out of Hades in seven places, creating an infernal maze.

The labyrinth motif appears nearly everywhere in the world; it can be found on carved bowls and on figurines from the Tisza culture in southeastern Hungary, which dates back to 5000 B.C. (see figure 6), and also in Native American basket weaving (figure 7). Labyrinths were also built into the floors of the great cathedrals of Rheims (see figure 6), Chartres, and Amiens (see

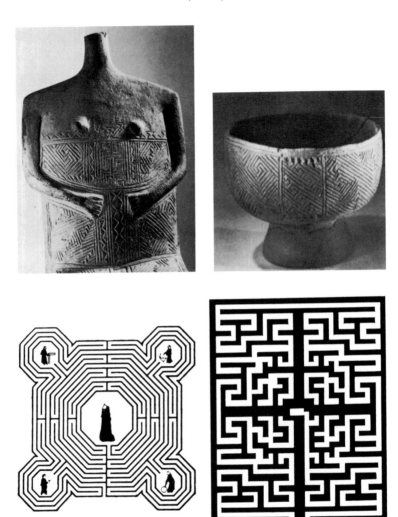

Fig. 6 The labyrinth—symbolic of a ritual descent into the earth—can be found on a statue of the Goddess (top left) and on a bowl (top right) of the Tisza culture (5000 B.C.) in what is now southeastern Hungary. Similar patterns are shown in a hedge maze from the Renaissance (bottom right) and in the floor plan of the cathedral at Rheims (bottom left), just outside of Paris.

figure 7), indicating that this initiation was absorbed by the Christian world.

In *The Divine Comedy*, Dante describes an initiation that parallels Christ's own journey from the depths of Hell up to the majestic firmament. This takes place in the three days between Good Friday and the Resurrection, a time of year when the entire world is poised between decay and regeneration. In the opening scene, Dante finds himself stranded in a dark and frightening place:

> Midway through life's journey I was made aware
> That I had strayed into a dark forest
> And the right path appeared not anywhere.
> Ah, tongue cannot describe how it oppressed,
> This wood so harsh, dismal and wild, that fear
> ... strikes now into my breast.

Dante goes on to confront the treachery of the world; we hear about wars and family deceits, about the arrogance of politicians and the hypocrisy of priests. By the end of this extraordinary work, however, he is no longer a fearful pilgrim who cowers at the entrance to the abyss. Instead, he is a man who has passed through the gates of Hell and interviewed its residents. With descent behind him, and categories of human suffering defined, Dante now ascends to Paradise and celebrates the beauty of the world: " ... my spirit in ecstasy was lost. ... What I saw seemed a smile of the universe" (canto XXVII).

We are called to make a similar journey in the course of our contemporary lives, though we have few courageous souls to guide us. In the twentieth century, our spiritual traditions have been completely sterilized and the darkness taken away. Christianity, as it is now popularly taught, gives us only half the story. We are told Christ himself went down into the center of the earth, yet we do not hear what occurred in those three days, even though we are dealing with an initiation powerful enough to change the history of the world.

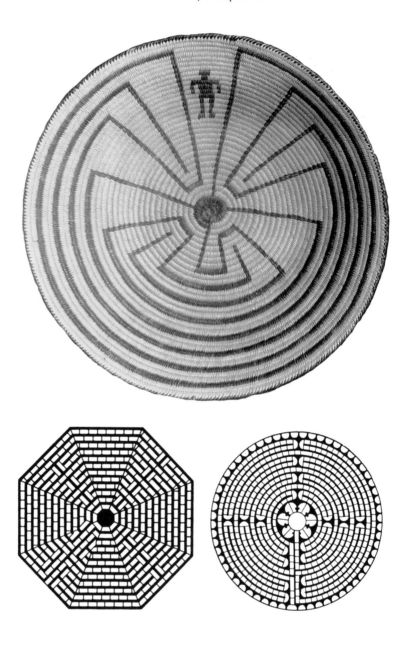

Fig. 7 *Mazes appear as the motif in this Pima Indian basket from Arizona (top) and also in the floor patterns of the great cathedrals at Amiens (left) and Chartres (right) in the north of France.*

Most of us want to jump over the most difficult part of the journey, which centers us on our suffering and on the inner darkness. This is to be expected in a youth-oriented culture. Yet the depths become more and more unavoidable as we move toward middle age.

When I was thirty-five, I surrendered to a long period of introversion; that winter I rarely turned on the electric lights; instead, I built fires and read books by candlelight. I went through my journals and recorded all my dreams, hoping to find a new direction in my life. By March, I had begun to profit from this inward turning. Where I had always forced myself to work so many hours a day, I now began to honor the dark side of the creative process, to give in to this period of inactivity, trusting that something new would eventually spring forth.

That Easter, our local church planned to hold a sunrise service out of doors in the old Dutch cemetery. I liked the idea of beginning Easter by honoring the darkness and its role in the creative process. My husband and I arrived promptly at 6:30 A.M., but found ourselves alone in the seventeenth-century graveyard. Wondering what had gone astray, we walked back to the chapel. The service had moved indoors because there weren't enough flashlights for the responsive reading. I began to see how dependent we are, in this tradition, upon *logos,* or the written word.

As we entered the church, a ceremony was being conducted by the youth group, which had chosen as the introit the Beatles' song "Here Comes the Sun." Young girls dressed like pink rosebuds then read from the Scriptures in breathless and barely audible voices. Here the new world was truly ushered in by virgin life!

Afterward, we attended a breakfast prepared by the youth group. As the pastor's wife came over to give us some news about the parish intern, our conversation was interrupted by a thunderous noise. The large commercial oven in the next room had exploded and for one frightening moment, everything stopped still. I thought, here is the darkness that was missing from the service. The loud noise was like the voice of the Divine, reminding us of the awe and terror that accompany rebirth.

I went home from the church breakfast, still feeling vaguely discontent. Though I was glad to be a part of the church community, something else was happening to me that year. I drew the curtains and went back to bed, wishing I could start the morning over. When my husband came upstairs to ask what was the matter, I cried out in a fury that surprised me: "Today is also supposed to be a celebration of the earth and of the feminine!"

I felt there was more to this day, and a crucial element had been denied. At one point in my life, I had studied the Christian mystics and even trained to become a spiritual guide. What I encountered in my informal practice were women who had been wounded by the church, who had left their own traditions because they could find no validation of their inner lives. That very weekend, I received a visit from a friend who was terribly depressed. She had found a rock in a nearby quarry and held it out to me, saying that it reminded her of a woman's torso with the top half torn away. This was how she felt: She was only half a person living in a culture that was oriented toward the masculine and that failed to recognize the body and the earth. I believe that many women become depressed at this time of year because our feminine rites of renewal have been securely locked away.

How could I begin to address this wound? That Easter I tried to improvise my own ritual. I asked my husband to help me celebrate the story of Inanna, which deals with the rebirth of the world. First, I set out two candlesticks on the floor of the meditation room. Then, I placed a white lily to the right, to represent spirit and the masculine, and a bright red amaryllis to the left, to honor the body and the feminine. I then laid out my collection of fossils and shells to symbolize the powers of the earth. The altar was now completely balanced, and I sat facing an old stone wall in our 1790 farmhouse in almost total darkness.

Though I had studied ritual for the last two years, I had never done anything quite like this, creating through my heart and intuition a service that would round out what I had always needed from the Church: a deeper acknowledgment of the feminine and of the germinating power of the dark.

I began to read aloud the story of Inanna and Dumuzi, which begins with a description of their union. Ninshubur, a faithful servant, leads the couple to their marriage bed, saying,

> My queen, here is the choice of your heart,
> the king, your beloved bridegroom.
> May he spend long days in the sweetness of your
>   holy loins.
> As the farmer, let him make the fields fertile,
> As the shepherd, let him make the sheepfolds
>   multiply
> Under his reign let there be vegetation,
> Under his reign let there be rich grain.
> In the marshland may the fish and birds chatter
> In the canebrake may the young and old reeds grow
>   high
> In the steppe may the mash-gur trees grow high
> In the forests may the deer and wild goats multiply
> In the orchards may there be honey and wine,
> In the gardens may the lettuce and cress grow high
> In the palace may there be long life.

This is the ceremony that inspired the Song of Solomon, and it is a most exquisite portrait of the link between human love and the vitality of the natural world. The passion of Inanna and Dumuzi quickens the heartbeat of creation, and the human heart becomes one with the world-pulse; its blood intermingles with the sanguine flow of all creation.

This union brings a period of fertility and abundance. Yet after a while, the balance must shift, and we must enter the stage of death and decay. In our story, the change comes about this way: Inanna goes to the Underworld to see her sister, Ereshkigal, who has lost her husband. Ereshkigal is in a rage, and so she strings Inanna up on the death pole and begins to torment her. Finally, the god Enki sends two flies to comfort Ereshkigal. (In Sumer, the fly was known as the carrier of the soul.) These tiny creatures commiserate with her as she moans, "Oh, my insides. Oh, my insides!"

Ereshkigal lets her sister go because at last she has an acknowledgment of her own pain and suffering.

Ereshkigal challenges us all to be this real: to face our losses squarely and to look death in the eye. When she asks, "Who is it that weeps with the Queen of the Underworld?" she means, "Who willingly surrenders to the great round of birth and decay?" Only when we know our place within this cycle is the stage set for reconciliation and release.

Inanna comes back to life and hurries through the gates of the Underworld, but she is only freed on one condition: she must send another down to take her place. The Underworld spirits follow her to see who she will designate. On the road back to the palace, Inanna meets her servant Nishubur, who convinced the god Enki to save her. Then she meets her two sons, who are dressed in mourning. Inanna will not condemn those who love and honor her. When she enters the palace, however, she finds Dumuzi eating a sweet fruit and sitting on the throne. He is so preoccupied with his feasting that he has not even noticed that the queen is missing.

"Take him!" Inanna cries, and Dumuzi is carried off to the dark kingdom of Ereshkigal.

At first, this seems nothing more than an act of retribution, but in truth it is the only way this union can be renewed: the king and queen must be equals in experience. The tale says both partners must face the darkness and reminds us that marriage cannot work if only one of the partners has been transformed.

Here the feminine is the initiator of consciousness. As I told this story to my husband, I honored a woman's ability to change the world. I also felt we balanced out the Easter message, which speaks of our redemption by the Holy Spirit. With this ritual, we recognized the transformation that occurs in the down-to-earth realm of marriage and relationship. Now we were in tune with both the heavens and the natural world.

Poet Judy Grahn has written a new version of this myth that shows how this initiation might take place today. It is about a woman who has forgotten that she is a goddess, even though she has all the beauty and the grace that once belonged to Helen of Troy. Our new Helen is a suburbanite with nice clothes, well thought of and admired, who has married "the right guy." Yet one day she tires of her perfect setting, and she ends up in "The Underworld," a bar full of unsavory people who tell her things about herself that she doesn't want to hear. Helen confronts those people she has always avoided on the basis of cleanliness and morality, and in the process, she reclaims the untold history of womankind.

First, she meets Penthisilea, Queen of the Amazons, and learns what it means to be a Warrior. Next, a chorus of women tell her about the time when feminine strength was worshiped. Finally, Helen meets a woman who is alone and vulnerable in the modern world. This woman is nearly killed by a gang of bikers—the perfect image for the violent masculine. The only thing that saves her is a chant—she begins to call out the names of all her friends and sisters. With this kind of incantation, the angry men disband and disappear. There is only one thing that can protect us: our ability to remember who and what we are.

This is the kind of work that every woman needs to do: make contact with her female ancestors and with their unsung strengths. After reading this story, I performed a ritual for all the female members of my family: I lit a candle for each woman and then named her special talents and abilities. I remembered each of these:

My great-grandmother Lotte, a farmer's wife who died while canning peaches at the kitchen sink at the age of ninety-four.

My grandmother Charlotte, a feminist, midwife, and trick-horseback-rider.

My aunt Elaine, who had four children and then died of a brain tumor at thirty-three.

My aunt Marion, who raised a daughter by herself, though she was legally blind.

My aunt Geri, who played her first piano concert on the radio at fourteen, then gave up her music to help run an orphanage.

My aunt Mabel, the church soloist.

My aunt Harriet, a national checker champion who lost her battle with leukemia at thirty-five.

My aunt Ruth, who was paralyzed on her left side after giving birth to twins.

My mother, Ruth, who worked so hard to give me music and art lessons, then projected her beauty and creativity onto me.

I acknowledged that I am the sum of all their efforts and my life is one place where their collective love and anguish can be redeemed. This is what Gloria Steinem accomplished with an account of her mother's mental illness ("Ruth's Song—Because She Could Not Sing It"); Judy Chicago, with her homage to women writers and artists ("The Birth Project"); and Alice Walker, in her essay on a woman's way of honoring the world

("In Search of Our Mothers' Gardens"). It is essential that we remember the lives of other women, even though this task will often take us to the Underworld of grief and despair.

In Judy Grahn's story, what gets Helen back from the Underworld before she sinks too far into this collective pain? A faithful woman friend, Nin (a counterpart of Ninshubur). Helen is rigid as a corpse because she has dared to look such suffering in the eye. This is just the right moment for an old companion to appear. The initiation process is finished, and to stay there any longer would be to risk a disintegration of the personality.

Helen arrives home in one piece and takes one look at her unsuspecting husband. All of a sudden he seems so naive, so *unknowing*. To remedy this situation, she sends him to the Underworld. This is what so many women do when they go through a profound inner transformation: they begin to will the same experience on their mates. If the man does not go to the Underworld of his own accord, they will torment him and carry out the work of Ereshkigal themselves.

Coming back from the Underworld is often the most difficult and dangerous part of the journey. A woman may shake up her marriage so severely that she has nothing left when she comes back to the light of day. We all need to have an experience of the depths, to go down into the dark and find out what makes things grow. Yet we must take care how we share the wisdom we have gained. Women may be the ones to initiate the transformation, but it is not possible for us to simply pass on what we have learned to our husbands and our friends.

When I first entered the Underworld of my emotions, I wanted my husband to experience my rage and disappointment. At times, I tried to impose my feelings on him, so I would not have to be in this dreadful place alone. Yet he was building up a business and needed to relate to the world in an entirely different way. I soon learned that husbands and wives must make their journeys separately and be careful to respect each other's timing. Too often one partner comes back from a confrontation with the underside of life with a preset ideology and begins to tell the other how to cope with his own transformation. Yet this is contrary to the laws of initiation. In the ancient world, these ceremonies were kept secret, and any revelation was punishable by death. We must remember that the Underworld experience is sacred and be sure not to drag another down there with us for our own private ends.

A man will proceed with his own initiation once he learns how to rely upon his *inner feminine,* and that is just what happens in our story next. When Helen sentences her husband to the Underworld he takes a woman with him. He goes on his descent with a girl who looks enough like him to be his twin. It is important to remember, however, that this is not a flesh and blood female but the "inner woman" who can put a man in touch with his own capacity for empathy and compassion. Because she is part of his own psyche, this sisterly companion can go to the Underworld for him and help him split the load.

Helen's husband needs to relate to this inner woman, for until now his life had been too one-sided. He was raised as the traditional male, and even his name is macho: Thomas Bull. As a scientist, he responds to all situations with cool objectivity. An astronomer, he contemplates his subject matter from a distance. He is man comfortable with boundaries, yet this story tells us that he must get closer to the feminine. Initiation must involve both halves of the personality, no matter what our starting point. While Helen goes down to the Underworld to bring together Beauty and the Warrior, Thomas must learn to join the Goddess and the Scientist. He must begin to value his own feelings and learn how to be at home within the body of the world. This is the goal of the descent for every one of us: to join earth and spirit, clarity and passion, and to lovingly embrace the opposites within ourselves.

As Carlo Gozzi observes, children "are made of amorous dough. As soon as they turn twelve, love has begun to take them somewhere. They see its glowing torch from afar and follow it through the half-light of childhood. . . . " At this time, everything exists in the realm of dream and possibility. What happens when young people have to come of age without the proper ceremony? How do they begin their love affair with life?

I have known two young people whose stories have touched me deeply in the past few years. "Susan," the nineteen-year-old daughter of a neighbor, was a model student, yet her grades suddenly dropped, and she became withdrawn and depressed. She aspired to be like her boyfriend who was studying physics at a nearby university. This young man had a strong analytical nature, and he wanted Susan to share his ideas and his scientific passions. The more she tried to do so, the more she felt phoney and inadequate. Like many young women, Susan felt she had to follow a young man through his rite of passage, and in the process, she ceased to believe in her own approach to life. Susan's depression lifted when she managed to affirm her own kind of creativity. She transferred to a fine arts college, where she began to paint and meet other people who affirmed her interests.

My other story is not so happy. It is about "Tom," a sixteen-year-old who was picked up for drug possession and for blasting trucks with a sawed-off shotgun while speeding down the local highway. Tom's parents married when they were in their teens and divorced when he was five. They are still blaming one another for their failed relationship and are also trying to shift the blame for Tom's addiction and arrest. The tragedy is that the parents are so preoccupied with their own problems they cannot help Tom find an answer to his most pressing question, Do I have the right to be alive?

Without initiation rites, we create a society that is run on the death instinct. Adolescents need a way to channel their new-found intensity; if they do not learn to celebrate life's mystery, they will be condemned to act out its tragedy. Erich Fromm states in *The Anatomy of Human Destructiveness,*

> Man cannot live as nothing but an object, as dice thrown out of a cup; he suffers severely when he is reduced to the level of a feeding or propagating machine, even if he has all the security he wants. Man seeks for drama and higher excitement; when he cannot get satisfaction on a higher level, he creates for himself the drama of destruction.

In adolescence, we are poised on the very edge of life, and we need certain rituals to ground us. When a friend asked me to help create a coming-of-age ceremony for her thirteen-year-old daughter, I began to think about my own adolescent transformation and the wisdom that I needed at that extraordinary time. "For every loss, there is a gain; for every death, there is a birth." These words might have comforted me as I thought about the changes in my body. I remembered how I lost my lithe and slender form and, with it, the ability to run off with the boys. The ripeness and heaviness of womanhood seemed so encumbering. At this stage, I needed to mourn the freedom I had lost. I also needed to embrace the company of older women and to learn their way of being in the world.

Because this initiation failed to take place, I remained fiercely competitive. At thirty-five, I was still trying to prove that I was able to keep up with the men. I was working nonstop to put out a monthly magazine and taking graduate courses in counseling. Then all of a sudden my body rebelled: I was immobilized for several months by a spate of viruses and infections. As I lay in bed recovering, I had a series of dreams about the initiation that I had been denied. They took me back to my high school days to help a young girl who, in my dreams, seems lost and confused. In the first dream,

I am in the office of a high school guidance counselor, being introduced to a young woman with
dark hair and a strangely impassive face. We are
supposed to get to know each other.

She hands me a children's picture book on cats. I
point to the illustration on the back and say,
"That's just like my Zoe." (I have such a cat whose
name means "indestructible life.")

I want to give this young woman a gift, but I
don't know what she likes. "I'll bet you like mysteries!" I offer. But she wants a book called *The Seasons*.

I decide to come back to this school again, only
next time I will be in a position of authority.

I notice right away that this poor young woman has very little
to sustain her. At first, I am even ashamed to be with her, but
when she shows an interest in Zoe (an interest in life) I decide
to be her friend. It is significant that I misjudge her at the
beginning, thinking she wants a novel of adventure when what
she really requires is a new relationship to nature. The book
she asks for is called *The Seasons*, and from this it is clear that
an understanding of these cycles will help her to live in a more
balanced way. This young girl is really a part of me: I, too,
must spend time with the animals and the seasons and learn to
trust my instincts. The dream is clearly offering guidance since
it takes place in a counselor's office. It helps me understand the
psychological component of my illness: if initiation does not
take place at adolescence, we must face this dammed-up energy
in the second half of life.

At first, I approached my healing the wrong way, making
detailed lists of how to change my diet and my schedule and
trying to jam too many "therapies" into a single day. Then
another dream spoke about my need to slow down and relax:

I am called to see a school principal. He points to a
pair of black horn-rimmed glasses with gemstones

all over them that sparkle like diamonds. They seem magical and are vibrating. He asks, "Can you identify these?"

"Yes," I say. "They are *being in the moment.*"

The glasses, of course, represent the feminine way of looking at the world, with the goal of being, rather than doing. This new attitude is as precious to me as a diamond; it is what will put the magic and vitality back into my existence.

I began to feel more in touch with the feminine the more time I spent in nature. My husband and I had moved to an old farmhouse on an estuary in upstate New York, and every day I sat on a glass-enclosed porch, watching the world unfold around me. In the early morning fog, I saw the deer walk across the mud flats; then the heron and the egret came down to explore the black bottom of the riverbed. By midafternoon, the tide had changed and the water was deep enough to swim across. The banks were inhabited by muskrat and beaver and the creek was filled with carp. As I began to dream about my surroundings, these creatures helped me to affirm my connection with the living world.

First, I dreamed that I was a golden fish with a human face and a human nervous system. Though it seemed regressive to be transformed into a fish—a kind of backward sliding on the evolutionary scale—I knew something important was happening. It felt as if I were reconstructing my personality from the ground up and learning how to reconnect with the wisdom of the animals. The fish taught me how to slow down and go with the tides. There was little sense in struggling upstream in my condition; I had to learn to surrender to these organic rhythms if I wished to find the strength to heal.

Next, I had a dream about a deer that would lead me to a new understanding of my femininity:

I am in a room with my mother and an older friend. There is a deer's head breaking through the

wall. The two older women caution me not to get
too close to it. But I am aware this is the Goddess,
so I kneel down in front of it and look her directly
in the eye.

In earlier cultures, the deer was sacred to the feminine. It
once belonged to Artemis, the goddess of nature, healing, and
childbirth. In the dream, my mother and her friend are afraid
of this ancient power and warn me not to get too close to it. I
began to see that my mother and her friends were cut off from
their roots in the earth. They had their babies in hospital rooms
and raised their children on formulas and frozen foods and
moved to the nature-free suburbs. I could not blame them for
failing to give me the initiation that I needed. I could, however,
begin to create one for myself.

After this dream, I set up a ritual to honor my connection to
the animals and the landscape. In a spare room that overlooked
the garden and creek, I laid out a sacred circle, some five feet
in diameter, composed of heron feathers, stones, a bird's nest,
and a heart-shaped bone I found in the woods. I sat in the
middle of the circle and called on the deer and the heron, the
beaver and the muskrat, the shad and the carp. I then asked
them to teach me about their ways of being in the world. The
deer spoke to me of trust; the heron, of purity of heart. From
the beaver and the muskrat, I learned tenacity, and I received a
lesson in surrender from the shad and carp. After doing this
ritual for a while, I began to see that a human life is not a
singular occurrence but the culmination of many earthly histories. The beauty and the grace of the animals are alive within
us, and the body and the brain that we inhabit recapitulate the
wisdom of the land.

A short time after this, I had a dream that offered me a
blueprint for my healing:

I am in a vast and ancient land, sitting with an old
woman who is a healer. She puts heat on my sore
body and rubs me down with herbs.

There are many people with flowing robes approaching from on a distant plain. But the old woman sits quietly and beats out a rhythm with a stone. There is a sacrificial animal hanging from a spit, and I listen to the click, click, click of the stones.

I ask why so many of the people are gathering now. She says, "Just to sit and pray. There is nothing more that we can do."

In the bushes, we see three huge, black water buffalo. We are in awe of these creatures and stay very quiet.

Suddenly, one is charging, and I know he has come for me. I decide not to run. I calm my breathing and remind myself that all animals are a part of me. The buffalo then turns into a shaman with a buffalo head who dances for me.

He points to the fire and says that it gives life to all things—even to the stones. He says I cannot eat anything that has passed through this fire without a special ritual. Otherwise I will be burned.

As he disappears into the sky, he tells me, "The wind will blow through your house, but do not be afraid."

In this dream, I meet the Old Woman and the Buffalo Shaman, two wisdom figures who urge me to take care of my body and to bless the food I eat. They assure me that I will be supported by nature. And they tell me that illness arises when I am too willful and attempt to impose my own ideas on the world. The message is "Let go of your expectations and your need to control. Let the earth receive you and let the winds blow through you, and you will be cured."

At present, we are so fascinated with the speed and facility of the intellect that we easily dismiss the feedback of the body and the earth. In this case, illness appears as a corrective, a way of slowing down the mind. While our ancestors went down into caves and labyrinths to affirm their connection with the material world, we begin our dialogue on the level of the body. In modern times, our cells become the crucible in which we are reconstituted and reborn.

When I was facing my own descent into the body, I desperately needed a guide. I found one in the Jungian analyst Marion Woodman, who wrote about her own physical crisis in *The Pregnant Virgin* and who understood that the body can become a powerful catalyst for psychological rebirth.

Woodman made a trip to India in the 1970s and went into culture shock as she walked through Delhi's black market, encountering beggars and homeless waifs. She had entered the Underworld where death and decay were visible on the city streets. Her distress was so apparent that one day a stranger stopped her in the marketplace and told her to go home. Woodman was determined to face the underside of life and not flinch or run away. At this point, however, her body reacted violently. She came down with a fever and with a bout of dysentery that kept her confined to her hotel room for a period of nine days. "We are each thrown into our own fire and the room in the Ashoka Hotel was mine," she writes, "There was no one to phone, no one to visit, nothing to do. All escapes were cut off. I had to move into my own silence and find out who was in there. . . . Gone forever was the world I had lived in. Without consciously knowing what had happened I had sacrificed my former system of values. . . . Either I had to flow with what life presented in the instant or I could not survive."

When Woodman lay crumpled on the floor, she realized she had never felt at home in her body. As the daughter of a minister and as an academic, she had learned to honor the realm of the spirit and the intellect. Now she would also have to come to terms with the physical world.

In the first days of her recovery, Woodman sat for a few hours in the hotel lobby; she took a place on a large red sofa in the middle of the room and was joined by an Indian woman in a flowing sari. This visitor kept pushing up against her until their bodies were touching. One day a man came up to Woodman and explained, "I sent my wife to sit next to you because I could see that you were very ill. Her body has helped to give you energy. Since you are better now, we will not have to come again."

Imagine a culture where a woman comes to offer you the energies of life! When Woodman was willing to accept the healing power of the body and the feminine, a stranger came to nurse her back to health again.

The second stage of Woodman's initiation took place a few days later during a taxi ride to the caves of Malabar. It was Krishna's birthday, and people poured into the streets to celebrate the regeneration of the world. Suddenly, out on the road came a cow with turquoise horns. The taxi driver swung the car into a ditch, and a group of men took Woodman's camera, her sandals, and her purse. They then lifted her up above their heads and carried her to an altar. What happened next is so extraordinary I will let her tell you in her own words:

> Convinced that I was about to be sacrificed, I was
> simultaneously dead and fiercely alive, quite beyond
> fear. I was receiving powerful energy from the men,
> a comingling of love and praise and awe. A man
> who seemed to be a priest put grass in my mouth,
> chanting with the others. He prayed over me. He
> took the grass and divided it up among the men
> who ate it as if it were holy grass. They picked me
> up, put me on the altar, and chanting, did a slow
> dance around me.

After this impromptu ceremony, she was given back her sandals, her camera, and her purse. In a few moments, her driver reappeared, smiling, and took her back across the fields.

What must it be like to wake up in the middle of another culture and be honored as a goddess? When we have the courage to descend into the dark side—and to face our fears and hatred of the body—unimaginable things take place. A teacher from Canada becomes the holiest of holies, and takes part in a celebration of rebirth.

Another writer, Eleanor Munroe, reminds us that India worships the earth as a goddess and the people pray to her many times a day. Little clay shrines to the Mother can be found at the foot of trees, in open fields, along highways, or in the lobby of a skyscraper:

> In this ecosystem the earth is a living member that the Hindu devotee calls Mother India. She can be seen on a map, lying on her back, her head in the Himalayas, her feet amid the triple seas—the Arabian Sea, the Indian Ocean, the Bay of Bengal. Her children have only to dip up a palmful of water out of any free-flowing brook or spring-fed tank to drink of her life-supporting fluid.
> ... "If a hairsbreadth separate you from the Universal, you suffer anxiety," says a respected Hindu psychoanalyst. Then the cure for anxiety, as for all other woes attendant on material life, is to sink one's flesh back into the flesh of the Universal Mother.

We in the West need to be initiated once again into the mysteries of the earth. We need to descend into these sacred places—into rivers, caves, and labyrinths. There we will learn how to leave behind our cares and grievances and find our solace in the body of the world.

DESCENT INTO THE MOTHER

The fear of woman and the mystery of motherhood have been for the male no less impressive imprinting forces than the fears and mysteries of the world of nature itself.

—Joseph Campbell
The Hero with a Thousand Faces

OUR FEAR OF NATURE RUNS SO DEEP BECAUSE IT IS tied to our very first experience of the mother. In my earliest memory, my mother is bending over me in the half light of the bedroom, her face round as a moon. She takes me from the crib and cradles me in her arms, then begins to hum a gentle lullaby. I am surrounded by her sounds, her body, and her breath and secure in the belief that our contact will be continually renewed. A few nights later, I cry out for her and am met only by the darkness. I yell louder and try to expel this awful longing from my chest. Then suddenly she appears, her smile distorted, her face no longer round and smooth. The hands that used to open and receive me now are tightly clenched. In an instant, my mother turns into the enemy. From now on I do not know which face to expect: the one that destroys and annihilates or the one that nourishes and provides for me. This is the memory we all have in common—the moment in which we realize there is no guarantee of safety in the body of the mother or the body of the world.

"Safety" is something we must create by and for ourselves. In childhood, however, we do not have the ability to do this. We are so dependent on the body of the mother that she seems to be an extension of nature with all its awesome powers. We see her, not as a mere human, but as the "World Mother who represents the poles of life and death," and we fear that we will lose ourselves in her eternal round. The *Nirvana Tantra* states unequivocally that, in the beginning, all was feminine energy: "Compared with the vast sea of the being of Kali, the existence of Brahma and the other gods is nothing but such a little water as is contained in the hollow made by a cow's hoof. Just as it is impossible for a hollow made by a cow's hoof to form a notion of the unfathomable depths of a sea, so it is impossible for Brahma and other gods to have a knowledge of the nature of Kali."

This all-consuming Mother appears in many cultures as a two-sided figure capable of both creation and destruction, of nurturing and annihilating (see figure 8). When we give ourselves over to the mother we have no individuality, no consciousness. That is why separation from the mother is a major theme in world mythology.

Tribal cultures know that the dark side of the feminine can overpower us and hold us back from life. Anthropologist Mircea Eliade describes the separation rites of one Australian tribe in which a boy is literally dragged away from the mother's hut by two strong men. "These guardians prepare his food, bring him water and instruct him in the traditional myths and legends, the powers of the medicine man, and his duties to the tribe. One night a great fire is lighted and the guardians carry the novices to it on their shoulders. The novices are told to look at the fire and not to move, no matter what may happen. Behind them their mothers gather, completely covered with branches. For ten or twelve minutes the boys are 'roasted' at the fire. When the chief medicine man considers this first ordeal has lasted long enough . . . the bull-roarers are sounded behind the row of women. . . . The women [then] retire a few miles away where they set up a new camp. The first initiation ceremony, comprising separation from the women and the ordeal by fire, is thus completed." The "roasting" burns away the protection of the mother and allows the boy the freedom to puruse his own identity. After the women are sent away, the boys begin to grow "a second skin." That is, they enter the world of the fathers and learn how to live as men.

Fig. 8 *The two faces of the Mother are shown in this terra-cotta figurine of Mexico (ca. 1200 B.C.). Such clay figures were buried with the dead as an assurance that the maternal powers of the earth would receive their departing spirits.*

The Wiradjuri, another Australian tribe, effect this separation in a similar way. Says Eliade: "The novices are seized by their guardians and carried off to the forest where they are daubed with red ocher. . . . A group of men arrives from the direction of the sacred ground, beating the ground with rods and throwing burning sticks. Meanwhile other men quietly seize the boys and lead them some distance away. When the women and children are allowed to look, they see nothing but ashes and burning sticks all about them, and they are told that Daramulun [the male creation god] tried to burn them when he came to take the novices."

Clearly, this ceremony has a great effect on the mother, preparing her psychologically for the loss of her son. Eliade concludes: "What we have is a break, sometimes quite a violent break, with the world of childhood—which is at once the maternal and female world and the child's state of irresponsibility and happiness, of ignorance and asexuality. The break is made in such a way as to produce a strong impression both on the mothers and the novices. In fact, in the case of nearly all Australian tribes the mothers are convinced that their sons will be killed and eaten by a hostile and mysterious divinity whose name they do not know, but whose voice they have heard in the terrifying sound of the bull-roarers. They are assured, of course, that the divinity will soon resuscitate the novices in the form of initiates."

In some tribes, young boys are even permitted to strike their mothers and to manhandle them in a show of ritual aggression. Later, the adult males of the tribe cut their own penises, and the boys must drink this blood from the phallus. This marks a major transformation. The boys have come from the blood of the mother and were sheltered in the womb; now they are born from the blood of the father, and at this point, the men tell them about the mysteries of procreation.

These rites take place at the stage when young boys are growing very conscious of their sexuality and more and more fascinated with the body of the mother. Incest taboos are aimed at releasing this energy and redirecting it toward the good of the whole community. Eros is no longer dominated by a wish to possess the parents. Instead, it becomes a feeling of responsibility for the outer world.

Separation from the mother is the key to claiming our own creative energy. Without it, we remain blocked and our full potential unreleased. As C. G. Jung said in *Aion,* a man who does not complete this separation will be unable to act as the carrier of life. When a man is stuck in this regressive place, his eros remains "as passive as a child's for he hopes to be caught, sucked in, enveloped and devoured. He seeks, as it were, the protecting, nourishing, charmed circle of the mother, the condition of the infant released from every care, in which the outside world bends over him and even forces happiness upon him." A young man must learn to seize his own kind of happiness. If not, he will be part of a secret conspiracy between mother and son where each helps the other to betray life. The unconscious mother sees nothing wrong with this: She ruthlessly pursues her need for union, and it is no wonder that in tribal rites, the young man's energy must be literally *stolen* by the men.

This separation is not any easier for us in modern times. Even the most educated and rational men may remain stuck in the mother and continue living out this symbiosis. Indeed, analyst Marie-Louise von Franz warns that their apparent "reasonableness" may be a trap. "A man cannot escape possession [by the Mother] by intellect alone," she says. "We have only to remember Oedipus. He cleverly answers the riddle of the Sphinx sure as he has outwitted the eternal feminine. But in the end, he marries his mother anyway."

Many of us are sure that we have broken free, yet our achievements in the outside world only mask our true dependency. We may be enmeshed in Mother-Institution—in Mother-Corporation or Mother-Church—and then retire to the safety of the Mother-Wife. The point of the Oedipus myth is that there are no quick routes to release. We try to recreate this union, because a part of us still wants to be nourished and protected. When we feel fragmented and alone, we fantasize a return to Eden and to the paradise of the earth-womb. Otto Rank has written, "At the back of the Oedipal saga there really stands the mysterious question of the origin and destiny of man. . . . Oedipus' blindness represents a return into the darkness of the womb, and his final disappearance through a cleft rock into the Underworld expresses once again the same wish to return to the mother earth." This desire is regressive because we want others—whether human beings or institutions—to create this paradise for us. What is the key to redemption? We must break from the personal mother, reverse the tide of longing, and redirect it toward the living world.

Several years ago I had the privilege of witnessing and participating in a male initiation rite at a workshop in upstate New York. A man in his early forties, whom I'll call David, stepped forward and began to tell his story: for years he and his brothers had remained overly attached to their mother. Now that she was dying of cancer, she was still controlling the entire family from her hospital bed. David now asked our group to help him create a ritual to help him separate from the devouring feminine.

First, the workshop leader gave David a tennis racket and asked him to strike a mound of pillows with all his strength. Then he was told to address his mother as if she were right there in the room and tell her that he wanted to claim his masculinity. A body of women then lined up in front of David like a Greek chorus and gave voice to her controlling nature. "You're mine," the women said. "I own you, David. You'll never be free to marry. You still belong to me."

David continued to beat the pillows until he was physically exhausted. Then, at one point, the men came up and gently surrounded him. They began to move in a circle and to moan and wail as if they were in mourning. Then their feet moved faster, and their voices rose, until they whirled across the room in an ecstatic dance. For a moment he was free! They were free! Then suddenly there was silence.

The workshop leader asked, "Why did you stop? I know you were afraid. But that is your masculine energy. You must learn to contain it." This exercise was very difficult, and I began to see it is not the separation we find so hard to bear but the process of reconnecting to the life force. We have developed many ways to deal with our pain and loneliness, yet we do not know how to handle the pleasurable sensation of being fully alive and fully in ourselves. For many of us this remains a dizzying and dangerous possibility.

We have long known that separation plays a big part in masculine psychology. We have only recently begun to recognize that women, too, need to break away from the safe enclosure of the family and the domination of the Mother archetype.

I had always thought of myself as an independent woman. I left home at eighteen and put myself through college. When my father died soon afterward, I promised to look out for my mother. At first, I did so from a distance, offering advice and financial support. Later, I helped her through a major illness and became more personally involved. I saw myself as the caretaker and grew accustomed to this role. When, at thirty-five, I wanted to marry and start a family of my own, something held me back, and I did not understand the problem until I had the following dream:

> I am getting married today. There is a big room underground, where I am getting dressed. All the older women are helping me with my gown. I want to wear a bright sash with flowers embroidered on it, but they tell me it is not appropriate. After they leave, I tie it on so you can see a dark plum color at my waist.
>
> As I emerge from this cavelike place, I see some guests standing in the stairwell. I go back into the depths and hide until they go away. Then I come

out to look at my wedding cake. It is huge, with
icing on it that looks like black bear fur. I can't believe the caterer has come up with this!

In the beginning of the dream, I am being told by the older
women how to dress, yet I want to do things my way, so the
wedding reflects something of my own personality. That is why
I turn the sash around, so there will be some color showing on
my gown. I then hide in this underground cave until I can come
out without being seen or recognized. In this very private moment, I begin to contemplate the wedding cake. The bear fur is
an ingenious image, a message from the unconscious that shows
I am in need of separating.

In earlier cultures, the bear was invoked in initiation rites as
a substitute mother and as the protector of young girls. The
word *bear* has always been connected to mothering and birth
and is the source of our expression "to bear a child." Although
the bear is considered the most nurturing of animals, she eventually leaves her cubs up in a tree and walks away from them.
This is a brutal separation, yet necessary for the young to develop their own survival instincts. My dream takes place in a
cave very much like a bear's den. It shows me that I have to
leave the mother's realm and learn to make my own way in the
world.

Freud once remarked that the communication between mother and child is almost telepathic. The emotions of the mother
go directly into the daughter as if they were connected by a
kind of psychological umbilicus. It is this cord that we all have
to cut. One day, I spread all my ritual objects on the floor,
laying out my rocks and shells, my heron feathers and deer
bones. I saw this circle as a boundary between myself and my
mother. Then I took the sharpest stone in my collection and
cut that imaginary cord that bound me to her at the waist. As
I made this severing motion, I thanked my mother for her love
and guidance and prayed for the strength to invent my own
kind of femininity.

I have done this ritual of casting the circle many times, and each time I remind myself that I have a responsibility, not only to my mother, but to the energies of life. Curiously, this has made it easier for me to treat her with understanding and compassion. When I was still dependent, I tried to control her responses and emotions. I wanted her to be strong and perfect so she could pass these feelings on to me. Now she is free to be human, to have her own fears of growing older. To this day, our relationship is enhanced whenever we are strong enough to acknowledge our separate ways of being in the world.

Initiation rites help us to move away from the personal mother and from the dissatisfactions of our childhood. We need these ceremonies if we are to leave behind the disappointments of the past and learn to take our nourishment directly from life itself. Without this kind of grounding, we will put more and more pressure on relationships. We will ask others to provide us with the basic sense of security and self-worth. We will remain in our infantile dependency and try to find our own meaning in and through the lives of others. This prayer of uncertain origin addresses our need to leave the safe haven of the family and find our mother and our father in the body of the earth:

> I have no father
> Thou art my father
> I have no mother
> Thou art my mother
> I have no relations
> Thou art all my relations
> I have no home
> Thou alone art my home
> I have no friends
> Thou art my friend

I have no ambition
Thou art my ambition
I have no desire
Thou alone art my desire
I have no life
Thou art my life
I have no mind
Thou art my mind
I have no goal
Thou art my goal
I go to the Imperishable Treasure
And I go and I go and I go . . .

The family provides us with our first connection to the generative powers of the cosmos. Beyond that is a universal family we must recognize as we learn to take our mothering and fathering from a deeper source.

Tribal cultures are much better at this, and they routinely honor the "world parents" in many different ceremonies. A particularly beautiful one is performed by the Laguna Pueblo to bless the building of a home. One elder explains in *Respect for Life:* "The Laguna tribe has always understood this earth to be its mother so we relate everything back to it [in the construction of a home]. A request is first made to White Hands . . . a religious person who prays all day long prior to making his assignment of a home. After White Hands has blessed the site, the whole family gets together to pitch in and help. These buildings are sacred and we treat them as such. The four walls represent the four seasons as well as the four corners of the earth. Like the Plains Indians, my people also treat the home as a woman because it is made from Mother Earth."

Men and women share equally in the building so the creative powers of the World Mother and the World Father will be equally represented. In this way, the people take care to balance both male and female energies. In this cosmology, parents are "transitional objects" that bring the child into a full relation with the living world. The Pueblo are not afraid to lose the mother and the father, for they will find them once again in their surroundings.

In our society, this initiation fails to occur, and so we project our fury on the natural world. We very naturally expect to receive these teachings from our parents and our culture. When we don't, we begin to treat the environment with hostility and contempt. In our narcissistic rage, we would destroy the Mother Planet and yet preserve our own inventions. This is the twisted logic of the neutron bomb. Yet we cannot expect the world to continually cope with our aggression. The earth is not the proper target; in fact, she is the only safe mother because she makes no personal demands.

One of the main goals of psychotherapy is to help us repair our bond with the feminine and nature. The British writer and counselor John Rowan speaks candidly about the rage and anxiety triggered by the feminist movement in the 1970s. Men began to feel overwhelmed by women and to see the Devouring Mother everywhere. In *The Horned God*, Rowan describes what happened in his own life at the time:

> In 1975 a whole new dimension appeared in my relationship with feminism. I had been working in my therapy on various aspects of a horrible female figure I called Big Granny who was full of hate for me. In April I had a long therapy session where I quite spontaneously went back to my own birth and relived it, discovering that I had hated being born, hated being weaned, and hated my mother for separating from me. I had decided to get revenge on my mother.
>   . . . [I began to see] that all the hate I had experienced from my Big Granny fantasy figure was actually my own hate projected onto the outside world.
>   After that I had resolved . . . to be independent, to not need women or anyone else. My need for revenge spread until it included all women and all

men, too. In reality I hated everyone. But in particular, and most of all, I hated my wife.

When men are not reconciled with the Mother, any woman
can trigger their suspicion and mistrust, and the one who suffers most is usually the wife. In this case, a man must remember
that he is not dealing with a flesh and blood female but with
an archetype. The Terrible Mother is not personal but a destructive energy that permeates the world. Rowan advises men
that they must distinguish between her and the individual woman if they wish to heal:

> Through therapy I was able to give this up. I was
> able to forgive my mother, and to forgive myself for
> making such a mistake. My whole attitude to wom-
> en started to melt and change. When I told my wife
> I had made this amazing discovery, that deep down
> I hated her, and was in effect using her to get re-
> venge . . . she expressed no surprise, except that it
> had taken me so long to discover it.

Sometime after this, Rowan was able to make contact with
the divine feminine. He began to read about the Celtic goddess
who presides over creation and destruction, and he had this
vision of her during meditation:

> In the circle of trees I sit down.
> Moving down to the centre
> The dark
> The lovely fearsome nourishing darkness
> Into Her realm, Her space, Her time.
> And then She is there
> My heart, Her heart, singing, wide open, full
> Her darkness, Her blood, Her power, Her changes,
> Her force, Her awe, Her strength.

Such a vision washes away everything that has gone before
and offers a moment of grace. It is a sign that a man has gone

through the full cycle of initiation, that he is able to receive the feminine as it is expressed within his own psyche and within the deeper cycles of the earth. He no longer clings to an idealized image of womanhood but incorporates the darkness. As Rowan said, this experience "was like finding a long-lost mother." Yet what he found was his mother *in* the earth itself.

What happens when our culture forgets about the feminine altogether and suppresses its dark powers? That question is addressed in the motion picture *Aliens*. In this compelling science fiction film, we see how the Negative Mother attacks us when we are least aware of her destructive energies. The Alien of the title is a giant insect, a Negative Mother who uses human bodies to incubate her eggs. She feeds off our life energy to keep her brood alive. When the embryos are ready to be born, the human host is brutally destroyed. There is a ripping of bones and flesh as the insect's head bursts through the chest cavity, puncturing the stomach and lungs. Significantly, these are two areas that are most affected by the mother complex. Breathing and digestion are impaired when the mother suffocates us and deprives us of the nourishment we need. When the heroine has to describe this awful creature, she says, "I don't know what the hell it is. It lays its eggs and then takes our bodies to survive. One thing is for certain: it destroys all human life."

Ripley is an officer who loses the entire crew of her spaceship to the Alien. She manages to escape and remain in hypersleep until she is found fifty years later by a scavenger ship. When she returns to Earth and speaks about this terrifying creature, she is labeled "crazy" and "insane." Stripped of her flight command, she is given the mundane job of loading cartons in a warehouse and told she must adapt to ordinary life. Yet the creature haunts her. She has bad dreams and night sweats. She chain smokes, and she cannot eat. This is the plight of modern women who have had a deep experience of the negative feminine—a real confrontation with the terror that exists in nature and at the core of life. At first, no one believes them. They are told that they are unstable and depressed. Everyone advises them, "Be a nice girl—then your bad dreams will go away."

Aliens expresses the underlying message of our culture: "Deny the terror. Push down your fear of the Devouring Mother. Repress the pain of death. If you don't think about these things, they will not exist." Yet when we deny these realities, we only make ourselves more vulnerable to them and our bad dreams return with increasing ferocity.

The people of the planet Earth know so little about these destructive energies because they are all unimaginative, cost-conscious bureaucrats. There are no more nations, just one massive institution called "The Company" that is comprised almost totally of men. The Company executives are experts in logic and efficiency. Not surprisingly, they refuse to believe that the Alien exists because it is too irrational. Instead, they insist that there are no demons, that the universe has been made safe and sterile for all time.

The few women in The Company have adopted the same mechanical attitude. They dutifully serve the bureaucracy by suppressing any thoughts or feelings of their own, and they dress like men, in suits and ties. In this unbalanced culture, there is no recognition of the feminine.

One day The Company loses contact with a group of colonists on a distant planet and begins to suspect that Ripley's story might be true. Soldiers are sent to investigate, and Ripley is allowed to go along as a consultant, though she has no real authority. In command is a green recruit from the space academy who is unprepared to deal with any real emergency.

As soon as they land, the soldiers find that the entire settlement has been destroyed. All the earthlings have been wiped out by the Alien—that is, all but Newt, an eight-year-old girl who has bravely hidden in the air ducts. While the brash young commander is impatient with Newt, Ripley is the one who comforts her. She does not lie to her and tell her that the universe is safe. Instead, she validates her terror. "I know," she says, referring to the creature. "I've seen it, too."

Later, the soldiers are wiped out by the Alien and Newt shows Ripley where the generator is and how to get to it by crawling inside the air ducts. Newt also knows the underground pathway to the launching pad and what time of night the creature prowls. By the end of the movie, there is a strong bond between Ripley and the girl. The Alien is the Bad Mother who destroys all humans, but Ripley emerges as the Good Mother who honors and protects new life.

During their escape, Newt falls through an air shaft and into the steamy basement where the insect lays her deadly eggs. Ripley goes down and torches this macabre nursery. Later, the insect forces her way inside the spacecraft to take revenge upon the human child. This time, Ripley straps herself into a "loader," a piece of machinery that amplifies her size and strength. Her body is now like a mechanical crane that can lift extraordinary weight, and with these added powers, she is ready to engage in a battle of the archetypes. In one breathtaking scene, we have the violent confrontation of the Good Mother and the Bad. Ripley ejects the Alien from the hull of the ship and sends her flying into outer space. The Devouring Mother is temporarily defeated—but she is still alive. This ending rings true psychologically—the Bad Mother has been beaten, but she cannot be destroyed. She will always be somewhere "out there," in the very fabric of the cosmos, ready to invade our lives, if she is not confronted consciously.

This film says that the Evil Mother must be recognized—or else we will be totally unable to cope with our surroundings. The material world will be devalued; we will run the planet like a warehouse and put a low priority on human life. In many ways, we are like the executives of The Company who do not want to face the possibility of death and destruction. We insulate ourselves from life with logic and with reason. And we try to reassure ourselves that the world is totally benign.

It could be said that the real villain in this movie is not the Alien but The Company. The insect is a purely instinctive form of life, and we must come to grips with it, yet The Company asks us to shut down our awareness. We cannot protect the earth if we fall into denial, any more than if we act from our own greed and self-interest. One Company officer, for example, wants to bring the alien embryos back home and market them. He does not realize how dangerous these things are; he thinks about a profit-making scheme to mass-produce them, though such an act could bring about the destruction of the universe.

Aliens shows us that it is possible to oppose the Negative Mother, to stand our ground and protect our own creation. We can emerge, like Ripley, on the side of life and birth. However, first we must overcome our cultural denial as well as our addictions to money and to reason. We can no longer depend on the blind assurances of The Company. Instead, we must value our own experience over anything put forth by the collective. Only in this way can we recognize the devouring energy that poses a real danger to the earth and to ourselves.

As people tried to make these distinctions in earlier times, they were guided by fairy stories and folktales. There the Negative Mother appears as the Old Woman or the Witch. Throughout, the crisis is the same: The Witch tries to steal our energy; she demands more and more of us until she drives us to distraction or to our death. She wants—and gets—transformation or extinction. If we stand up to her, she teaches us and gives away a portion of her power. If we cave in, she destroys us bit by bit.

Today, the Witch is far from dead. Indeed, she is behind all compulsive behavior, from eating disorders to addictions. Longings for food, alcohol, or the perfect love relationship are essentially longings for the primal state of unity with the Good Mother. In our present culture, *real* nurturing is in short supply, and so we begin to rely on toxic substitutes. Women with eating disorders are in constant conflict with the Mother. In an effort to disgorge her negative energies, they starve themselves. An anorexic is afraid of the feminine, and so she will refuse to eat or take her inner nourishment from any outside source. The bulimic sees food as the Good Mother and links it to the nurture of the Self. Yet once she has eaten the chocolate cake or the loaf of bread, she feels she has been cheated. She still feels empty inside, and so she throws up or gags herself. Both women are really starving for down-to-earth relationships and an experience of positive mothering.

The first step in healing is to recognize our fear and vulnerability, our need to feel safe in our surroundings. When we are stuck in the Negative Mother, our whole environment seems to be controlled by a demon or a witch. The following journal entry shows my own struggle to break free of this:

I am feeding the witch
who will not let my body speak.

Where does it go—
the stuff I cram down my stomach?
Into the jaws of the Devouring One.

I blast her off my belly
and send her flying to the ceiling.
Yet now the witch is dancing on my head.
We live together in a dusty cavern full of cobwebs.
Each day I hear her voice:
I put the furniture back
smooth the slipcovers
always pressing, cleaning
fixing up this awful place
never asking, Whose house is this anyway?

Each day
She asks me to make her Chaos
into sheer Perfection.

I've been told it's dangerous
for the witch to be transformed.
But is there any choice?
Shall I be baked in the witch's oven
and emerge one day
a confectionary witch myself?

My soft, round belly
will she be in there always?
Will I eat, eat, eat
to satisfy the witch
who wants more
than I can ever give?

Now I am alone in her white house
in the middle of the forest.
It is hard, keeping both feet on the ground
hard not to fly up the chimney to the head.

Yet, if I stay here long enough
maybe I can get my body back.
And the next few crumbs I eat
will be a thing of real communion.

Food cravings, in particular, have to do with our longing for
the feminine. We want to open up and use our bodies in a
sacred way, to reconnect with the Great Mother, that goddess
with broad hips who has the ability to contain men and babies
and the energies of life. Most women I know have, at some
time, used food as a substitute for this kind of femininity. I
have even done so in my dreams. In this one:

> I am attacking a large box of chocolates. There are
> many small square candies. At the center are two
> large round pieces shaped like breasts. I have eaten

all the others. Yet these are the ones I really want,
and there is no way to get hold of them!

The chocolates are not the most important thing. Rather, it
is the big, dark woman who is only barely visible in the dream.
She is a variation of the World Mother, the comforter, provider,
and protector. This is the positive energy we need, the loving
mother we must learn how to celebrate (see figure 9).

Ironically, our culture conjures up the Negative Mother by
asking us to live in such a disembodied way. Note the fears of
the anorexic: that the Negative Mother will destroy her body
by bloating it, fattening it, and making it unattractive. In a very
literal sense, the victim is forced out of her body and up into
her head. This is exactly what society does to women by ignoring their biology and asking them to adopt a highly rational
way of life. The Negative Mother emerges when no room is left
for spontaneity and we ignore the natural rhythms of our bodies and the earth. She is a warning that we are starving for real
and immediate contact with the mother and the body of the
world. She attacks us because we live too mechanically. Like
the people in the movie *Aliens*, we are vulnerable to the Negative Mother because our lives have become too abstract. We are
too spacey, too far out of our bodies, disconnected from our
feelings and our instincts.

Conscious rituals can surely help us to heal ourselves. We can
learn to be more aware of food and to bless the preparation
and the eating. This sacrament can and must be celebrated on
a daily basis; it cannot be saved for a formal mass or liturgy.
We need to support ourselves and celebrate our own renewal
right here and now. I recall the story of one overweight woman
who began to kneel before the refrigerator and bless every mor-
sel she put into her mouth. In a similar way, we all need to stop
and be aware of the psychic energy we are taking in. Does
it belong to the Good or to the Terrible Mother? We are
aligned with the Good Mother when we can affirm that every

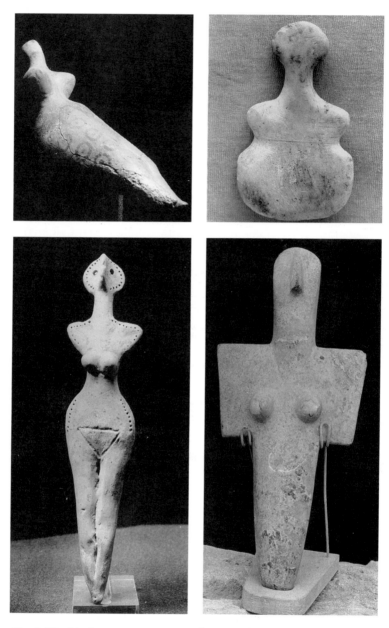

Fig. 9 *The Mother appears in many forms in these Stone Age sculptures. Early matriarchal cultures felt that all life sprang from the body of the Goddess.*

moment is an act of self-creation and a way of "re-membering" ourselves.

The Upanishads speak of the Kali Yuga—the age of the Dark Mother—when our own fertility wanes because we have damaged the fertility of the earth. There are many indications that we are in the Kali Yuga now. For one thing, women are reporting increasing difficulty with conception. As they behave increasingly like men, they find themselves cut off from their own biology. Though they may have been trained in the disciplines of law or economics, they have not been tutored in the ability to receive the energies of life. Research shows that professional women experience more difficulties during childbirth—perhaps because they are used to being in control rather than surrendering. As one expert observed, many women may have simply forgotten how to prepare themselves for this natural process.

Tribal cultures understand the link between our own creativity and the creativity of the land. If we harm the earth and strip it of its reproductive powers, we, too, will suffer. We must be grounded in a place, they say, just as a woman must be grounded in her body; nothing will happen unless we are connected to this vital core.

The African Ndembu believe that a woman is infertile because she has lost touch with the Great Mother and with the cycles of the earth. First, she is sent back to her own village; there her husband builds her a special hut where she will remain until she "regrows her womanhood."

To the Ndembu, to be barren is to "slip out of place" and forget one's attachments to the feminine and to the land. It is then that a woman is vulnerable to hostile spirits, especially the Mvweng'i, who presides over the initiation of young boys. The Mvweng'i represents a dangerous concentration of male energy, and the strings of his costume are believed to "tie up" feminine fertility.

In a sense, the modern woman also suffers from too much "maleness." She has stood too close to the fires of the spirit and sacrificed the wisdom of her body. She is out of touch with the earth and with her instincts. And she, too, needs a ritual to reorganize her energies. The Ndembu have a special ceremony to restore a woman to her self. First, they choose a site near the mouth of a river. Moving water must be found, for it represents the flow of life. Next, they dig a hole in the earth, signifying the womb that must be opened to give birth. As the water fills the opening, the woman lies down on the earth. She asks that a new life flow into her, and in this way, she aligns herself with the regeneration of the world.

Modern women must find new rituals to connect them with the source of all creation. If we do not have them, we will walk about with our energies dangerously uncontained. This lack of grounding will affect every aspect of our lives, not just child-bearing. If we do not develop our capacity to receive, we will never wholly open ourselves to the process of creation and never wholly understand the mystery of life.

It is true that our culture fails to honor the feminine and the earth. Yet there is only one solution—and that is to abandon our mechanical existence and begin to re-create ourselves. The novelist Margaret Atwood writes, "I have to recant, to give up the old belief that I am powerless. The word games, the winning and losing games are finished, at the moment there are no others, they will have to be invented."

To begin with, we must learn how to identify with the mothering that takes place in nature. A close friend told me how she experienced this reconciliation during the birth of her second child. Throughout the delivery, she felt held and mothered by the earth:

> It was mud season. On the day of the birth I awoke
> to a brilliant sun. The snow was melting and the

brook in our backyard had turned into a roaring river. Water was pouring down in rivulets along the walls bordering our driveway.

I walked in the woods behind our house for six hours until the birth was imminent. I felt like I had swallowed a hallucinogenic drug. Tiny buds had formed on the trees and water was dripping off them in the brilliant light. Each drop was like a separate crystal with hundreds of colors bouncing off it. The skunk cabbage had raised its head along the brook. The dark, oozing mud in the road seemed to be quivering.

I felt that the earth and I were giving birth together. I would stop during the contractions to take in long slow breaths and feel the running water and the sunlight enter my very being. I was in awe of those enormous forces which were operating both around me and in me simultaneously. I watched my belly move and felt as though I were watching a phenomenon of nature like a storm.

My friend had planned a home birth so she would be supported by her husband and her closest friends. Yet as she brought this child into the world, she found her source of inspiration in the land itself.

The Jungian analyst Christine Downing describes a stone figure of the Great Mother she discovered in a cave in southern California and then goes on to tell us about a ritual she improvised to honor her:

> Some friends had wanted to share with me a place sacred to them in the desert at the far eastern edge of the southern California county where I live. They left me to explore it in my own way, alone. I climbed up some cliffs and . . . some fifty feet from the summit was a small grassy plateau, just large enough for me to lie down in, completely ringed with low, flat boulders.
>
> Ritually, carefully, I took off my clothes and neatly folded them and lay down in the prepared space, aware of that wonderful sun in the sky above

> me, of the earth beneath my body, the encircling
> stones, the mountain behind me, the other moun-
> tains to my left and before me. I began caressing my
> body.
>
> Some while later, I sat up to look around me and
> discovered that behind the spot where my head had
> been laid was the opening of a cave. I moved to-
> ward it . . . and in the middle [was] the Stone
> Mother, Ungit, lying on her side, knees somewhat
> drawn up, with ripe, ripe breasts. Waiting. There
> was room barely for me to lie down beside her . . .
> and to feel myself in the Mother [and to know] the
> sweetness of woman with woman and the dark,
> dark mystery.

It is important for us to experience the Great Mother physically. When we do, we learn to love the earth and draw upon
her energy to nourish others. However, it is also possible to
embrace her in quiet meditation or in the privacy of our
dreams. I had my own vision of the Mother in this way:

> I dream that I am in a sacred temple deep within
> the earth. A woman in a white robe guards the
> flame, which is my soul. It is here that I must wait
> until I am told what to do in the outer world.
>
> It is warm inside, though the temple is made of
> stone. My hands grow hot; there is a fragrance in
> the air. I am there to be blessed, and I cry out soft-
> ly, "Mother, I have come home."

The rich mud of the earth, the stone figure in the cave, and
the white-robed woman in the temple—all are examples of the
Good Mother who nourishes and sustains us. She is the one
who can help us affirm our sexuality and who reminds us that
our lives are linked to the great life of the Earth.

Atonement with the Father

—————————— ❈ ——————————

The problem of the hero going to meet the father is to open his soul beyond terror [and] understand how the sickening and insane tragedies of this vast and ruthless cosmos are completely validated in the majesty of Being. The hero transcends life and for a moment rises to a glimpse of the source. He beholds the face of the father, understands—and the two are atoned.

—Joseph Campbell
The Hero with a Thousand Faces

FOR FORTY YEARS I HAVE BEEN TRYING TO UNRAVEL THE mystery of my father. He did not teach me how to *do* things so much as how to *save* things. Our attic, for example, contained two decades of newspapers he had neatly tied with string. In a box nearby was my father's red wool hunting jacket, thoroughly digested by the moths. There was a mason jar filled with stones and shells, a praying mantis skewered on a cardboard mount, a pile of photographs and some books my father had inherited from friends. He would often come upstairs and look at them, as if they were priceless treasures.

My father was a conservator of people, things, and history. Yet during adolescence, I rebelled against his knowledge and authority. When I came home from school, I turned on all the lights and left the house ablaze with electricity. This was my protest against his natural conservatism and his careful handling of resources. We grew estranged in those years, and then suddenly a heart attack put a halt to our relationship forever. Now here I am in middle age, wishing I could talk with my father and ask him how I might preserve the most important things in life.

Today there is so little chance for this kind of reconciliation. Indeed, the task of opposing and reuniting with the father has suddenly been eliminated. Fathers are seen as obsolete, irrelevant, uninvolved, or out of touch with "the real world." The psychoanalyst Alexander Mitscherlich describes this alienation in his postwar study *Society without the Father*. As we ignore the wisdom of our fathers, he says, we look increasingly to our friends for a sense of reassurance and self-worth. We reject the conservative values of our elders and refuse to measure ourselves against them. And in the process, it becomes less important to be competent and more important to be "liked."

In previous generations, the father would pass on his understanding of the world. He would instill us with a sense of meaning and of history; he would be the one to question our values and force our individuation. We have now replaced this bond with market surveys and the opinions of our peers.

As the writer Geoffrey Gorer observes, Americans have been particularly prone to reject the father and all outside forms of authority. As a nation of immigrants, we are ashamed of our fathers and of their connection to the past. And so we reject many of their customs and their values in an effort to assimilate. "The making of an American demanded that the father should be rejected both as a model and as a source of authority," Gorer says. "Father never knew best. And once the mutation was established, it was maintained; no matter how many generations separate an American from his immigrant ancestors, he rejects his father as an example and expects his son to reject him."

When we fail to honor the father, we are severely wounded. Our relationships are depersonalized, and we no longer act as the protectors and preservers of this earth. In *The Hero with a Thousand Faces,* Joseph Campbell reminds us the hero's journey is not an adventure for its own sake, nor is it related to secular stands of money and power. It is a search for the mastery of life that the father represents. The father is the one who enables us to branch out from the safe, enclosed realm of the mother and engage the world around us. He is a mediator between outward action and inner truth. He is the first objective "other" in our lives, the one who forces us to grow and develop, to leave behind our childish dreams. When the father is absent, as he is today, where do we turn for our salvation?

The wounded father-son relationship is an important theme in the *Star Wars* trilogy by Steven Spielberg and George Lucas. Like most young men today, young Luke Skywalker has never known his own father, yet he is smart enough to get his initiation from the last remaining Jedi knight. He also apprentices with Yoda, the wise old man, and learns to use the Force, the power that sustains all life.

When Luke comes of age, he leads a rebellion against the evil Emperor who has conquered and enslaved all other planets. The young idealist also finds out that he is the son of a fallen knight. Darth Vader is the Emperor's general and chief henchman, and his very name suggests the words *Dark Father*. Vader is encased in layers of black armor and is part man, part machine. He does not serve individual masculinity. Instead, he has sold his soul to "the Death Star" and become a part of a collective plan. That's why we never see his face; throughout, we only hear his ominous breathing through a metal mask. Every boy has a premonition that there is something evil and destructive in his father—yet as he matures, he must discover that he, too, has the potential to be a Dark Father and lose himself in the quest for power.

Luke takes on the evil Empire, but the outcome of this battle is not determined by brute force. Instead, it rests on a growing sympathy between the father and the son, and we learn that the battle with the dark side can be won only through acceptance and through love. Luke finds that he is able to read Vader's thoughts and also communicate his own. Through some kind of telepathy, Luke asks his father to give up control of the Death Star and help him set the people free.

At this point the Emperor intervenes. "If you will not embrace the darkness," he proclaims, "you will be destroyed." The Emperor is the Negative Masculine concerned with naked power. As he tortures Luke, he fails to see the emotion this arouses in the father. With his last remaining strength, Vader hurls the Emperor into the center of the Death Star. Then he removes his mask and shows his true face to his son.

While there must always be a confrontation with the father it does not have to be a fight "to the death." Instead, it can be a fight *for life*. In the process, we must give up our idealistic fantasies and see that we can be as hampered by our goodness as we are by the dark side. Revenge and hate can easily be constellated when one believes in the most heartfelt causes. In the beginning, Luke wants to create a better world, and he is willing to kill others to achieve it. The infantile ego craves perfection, but what happens if this perfect vision is denied? We rail against all forms of authority and are willing to risk the destruction of the universe just to prove that we are right. In this way, we take on the tyranny of the father and become the very thing we hate.

The demonic father is not just the stuff of science fiction. It is a short step from Vader to the Vaterland. Hitler was an Evil Father who tried to create a whole nation of obedient children. He offered them all the trappings of initiation; he created mottos, songs, and special uniforms for the young people but left out the most important element. There could be no confrontation with the Father, and hence, there was no way to come to terms with the energies of life. The German youth had no way to test their own humanity. Instead Hitler gave them permission to prey upon the wounded and the helpless and to claim their power in an *inhuman* way. This is the psychology of the fascist state.

The Tyrant does not always appear so much larger than life. In *To the Lighthouse*, Virginia Woolf shows us the controlling father in his socially accepted form. This time, there is no villain in black armor, only a middle-aged philosopher marching through the parlor in his shabby tweeds.

As the novel opens, the Ramsay family is settling into a vacation cottage in the Hebrides. The youngest son, James, is looking forward to the lighthouse journey. He sits nestled in his mother's lap, trying to decide what clothes to bring to the light-keeper's boy. Suddenly the winds change; they are coming from the west—an unfavorable sign. While James says the weather will clear, his father insists that it will rain. He keeps repeating over and over, like a cuckoo: "No going to the lighthouse, James." The boy is only seven, yet he is already engaged in an earnest battle with his father. We are told, "If there had been an axe handy, a knife or anything with a sharp point, [James] would have seized it and struck him through the heart."

The healing of this childhood incident does not take place until James is seventeen. By now, Mrs. Ramsay is dead, and they are finally going to make the lighthouse journey in homage to her. James has not forgotten the way his father crushed his enthusiasm some ten years before so he makes a silent vow. "Whether he was in a business, in a bank, a barrister, a man at the head of some enterprise, that he would fight, he would track and stamp out tyranny, despotism, he called it—making people do what they did not want to do—cutting off their right to speak."

Here we see how the son is wounded by the patriarchy. The father challenges him, and then stands squarely in his way. Eventually, a young man *has* to fight. If he doesn't, he will be plagued all his life by feelings of self-pity. At the most crucial moments, he will give in to his father's criticism. When he must act to preserve his land, his profession, his relationships, he will hear a negative inner voice saying, "You can't do it. It's no use."

These doubts are never completely vanquished. Even Mr. Ramsay wonders if his work will be remembered, if he has made a real contribution to the world of philosophy. To assuage his insecurity, Ramsay paces the front lawn and draws attention to himself, quoting lines of poetry. The family grows used to his sudden outbursts: "Someone had blundered!" "Stormed at with shot and shell!" When plagued by his fear of death, he speaks of drowning in a gale beneath the heavy waves ("But I beneath a rougher sea . . ."). What father has not played this role, ruining at least one memorable occasion with his own demands for praise and sympathy?

We learn, too, that James is angry because his father never praised him. On the lighthouse journey, he steers the boat angrily, wanting the recognition he deserves. Since Mrs. Ramsay is no longer there to diffuse their petty jealousies, the tension builds between the men as they move out into the open sea.

How is their relation finally redeemed? After a while, father and son begin to share the journey. There is a knitting together of their thoughts, and James finds that by some miracle, he shares his father's view of life. When he looks at the lighthouse, he sees in it "the loneliness that for them both was at the truth of things."

> So it was like that, James thought . . . it was a stark tower on a bare rock. It satisfied him. It confirmed some obscure feeling of his about his own character. The old ladies . . . [were] always saying how nice it was and how sweet . . . but as a matter of fact, James thought, it's like that. He looked at his father reading fiercely with his legs curled tight. They shared that knowledge. "We are driving before a gale and we must sink," he began saying to himself aloud, exactly as his father had said it.

At this point Ramsay's anguish and despair no longer seem to be mere theatrics but an accurate response to the trials and dangers of existence. James now understands his father's melancholy, for he, too, feels the sudden frailty of human life. At once, James is infused with a new sense of responsibility, and he begins to steer the boat with authority and confidence. At this point, his father also changes; Ramsay is no more the overweening tyrant but a vulnerable and timeworn man.

> He looked old. He looked, James thought . . . like some old stone lying on the sand.

As James docks at the lighthouse, Ramsay suddenly exclaims, "Well done!" His son has brought them through the most dangerous passage like a born sailor. In this moment, something extraordinary happens. Ramsay is free to behold the beauty of the landscape. He jumps up on the rocks, as though he has finally put down the burden of his anxiety and fear. As James takes on the role of protector, the transformation is complete: father and son discover a new relation to each other and to the energies of life.

Every generation must prove that it has acquired the necessary skill and patience to assume the stewardship of nature. Joseph Campbell liked to tell the story of Phaethon to illustrate this point. An ambitious lad, Phaethon wins a favor from his father Apollo and asks to drive the chariot that draws the sun across the sky. Apollo knows his son is too inexperienced to take on this important task. Yet he has no choice but to keep his promise. When the boy becomes frightened and drops the reins, the sun moves wildly through the sky. First, it dips too close to the earth and scorches it; then it reels too far away and a heavy frost kills the plants and animals beneath. Apollo is the god of moderation, yet now his son wreaks havoc with extremes. This story shows the value of withholding power until the young can do things right. Apollo and all other fathers must be assured that the young have conquered their ambition and are willing to respect the source of life.

In this day and age, we have so little time with the father and so little intimacy with nature. How, then, are men to understand their value as guardians of creation? Analyst Eugene Monick says that young men need a new appreciation of their bodies and of their own generative powers. *Phallos*, says Monick, is the essence of masculine creativity, yet it has been degraded and devalued in our modern age. Much older civilizations used to worship this kind of masculine energy (see figure 10) and honor it in their initiation rites. As a young adult, Monick dreamed that he and several other youths were lying on the earth in a great circle, their feet touching, with their hands on their own erect phalluses. When he became a psychoanalyst, he found that many other men had similar "initiation" dreams that urge them to reclaim their connection with their bodies and their instincts.

A few years ago, Monick and his teenage son made a pilgrimage to a Celtic shrine in Dorset to honor this kind of masculine energy. The Cerne Giant is a 180-foot figure with a phallus 35 feet in length (see figure 11). Carved into a chalky hillside two thousand years ago, this figure celebrates the male role in the regeneration of the world. Votive offerings were made to the giant up until the first century B.C., but many local residents are unaware of this imposing structure. Monick was fascinated by a group of young people who came across the giant unprepared:

> When my son and I came in sight of the Giant, a group of American teenaged bicyclists, male and female, simultaneously happened upon it . . . from the opposite direction. They slammed on their brakes. They could not believe their eyes. The girls held back as though embarrassed. The boys were excited. They [hopped] about like Mexican [jumping] beans, hooting, hollering, slapping each other on the back. Their response was almost as interesting to me as the Giant himself. . . .

The young men were astonished to see this symbol of manhood emblazoned on the ground so boldly. The girls held back, knowing that they were in the presence of a mystery they did not understand. Monick returned with his son the following day for a more private visit.

Fig. 10 *The phallus was an object of worship in ancient Greece. Large, white phalluses adorn the columns from the remains of a temple on the sacred isle of Delos, the legendary birthplace of Apollo (above left). Carved phalluses have also been unearthed on the mainland, at Tsangli, in Thessaly (above right). Another phallic shape (center) was found on an archaeological dig in the south of France and dates from prehistoric times. Also from the south of France, this double-phallus is assumed to be a carving from the head of a staff (bottom).*

Fig. 11 Celts sculpted the Cerne Giant into the landscape near Dorset, in Great Britain, sometime around 100 B.C. It represents the god Helith or his Roman counterpart, Hercules.

I climbed over the protective fence and trod upon
the outline of the phallos and testes. I sat down
upon the head of the phallos, as women used to do
when they wished to conceive.
  This was a connection with my phallos dream. It
was important for me to share this with my son in
a conscious way.

To care for the earth, says Monick, a man must have some
sense of his own generative powers. Yet modern men tend to
view themselves mechanically. They focus on their technical
performance as they pursue their favorite sports or attempt to
set new standards in their work. Their sexuality also becomes
a reflection of the need "to score" and to achieve. The question
men must ask themselves is this: How can masculine energy be
more related to the body, to the feminine, and to the natural
world?

Very early in his life, Jung had a profound experience of this
primal masculinity. In his autobiography *Memories, Dreams,
Reflections,* he recounts the following dream:

"I was in a big meadow. Suddenly I discovered a dark, rec-
tangular stone-lined hole in the ground. I had never seen it
before. I ran forward curiously and peered down into it. Then
I saw a stone stairway leading down. Hesitantly and fearfully,
I descended. At the bottom was a doorway with a round arch,
closed off by a green curtain. . . . I pushed it aside and saw
before me in the dim light, a chamber about thirty feet long.
The ceiling was arched and of hewn stone. The floor was laid
with flagstones, and in the center a red carpet ran from the
entrance to a low platform." Jung continues, "On this platform
stood a wonderfully rich golden throne. It was a magnificent
throne, a real king's throne in a fairy tale. Something was standing on it which I thought at first was a tree trunk twelve to
fifteen feet high and about one and a half to two feet thick. It
was a huge thing, reaching almost to the ceiling. But it was of
a curious composition: it was made of skin and naked flesh and
on top there was something like a rounded head with no face

and no hair. On the very top of the head was a single eye, gazing motionless upward. . . . The thing did not move, yet I had the feeling that it might at any moment crawl off the throne like a worm and creep toward me. I was paralyzed with terror. At that moment I heard from outside and above me my mother's voice. She called out, 'Yes, look at him. That is the *man-eater.*' That intensified my terror still more, and I awoke sweating and scared to death. For many nights afterward I was afraid to go to sleep, because I feared I might have another dream like that."

This image of the one-eyed phallus haunted Jung all through his childhood, though he did not speak of it until he was almost sixty-five. By then he had recognized the creature as a subterranean deity. During his childhood, Jung had great misgivings about this terrible god. Was the Lord Jesus, like the phallus, a devourer of little children? Would he give life or take it? Did the sacred masculine come to destroy or to create?

Much of Jung's work had to do with our ability to reconcile the Generative Father and the Terrible Father. He believed that both powers are necessary in the earth's eternal cycle of death and regeneration. He later wrote about his dream as an initiation rite: "The hole in the meadow probably represented a grave. The grave itself was an underground temple whose green curtain symbolized . . . the mystery of the Earth." In this vision, the archetypal masculine lies enthroned within the landscape and covered with green vegetation. Jung was finally able to see what lies behind the mystery: At bottom, the Great Mother and the Great Father are the same. They preside equally over life, and each has the power to seduce us into it or to deny us entry. As Jung discovered, we must pay homage to the World Parents if we wish to know the truth of things.

For a woman, the negative masculine is a composite of father, husband, institution, boss. He is the patriarchy that denies her inner meaning. He often shows up in a woman's dreams as a rapist or a murderer. Other times he may be a burglar—an appropriate metaphor since he's come to steal her energy. To claim her true self, a woman must disarm this inner figure and eventually befriend him. Yet at first, this seems to be a dangerous and impossible task.

When I was in my early thirties, I had a series of dreams about a gang of men who were trying to capture me and torture me. My crime was simply being female, and the underlying message was "You're not good enough." I kept trying to find out who their leader was, but he was always hidden in the shadows. The following journal entry shows my struggle to break free of him:

Who is it who controls my life
but will not show his face?
When I move
I hear him screaming, "Faster!"
and after that, "Not good enough!"

When I am happy he says
"You are about to be betrayed."

I want to get the bastard off my back
but he keeps hanging on.

What devil has got into me?
He doesn't want the spotlight for himself
he wants me to stand out front
and burn in the harsh glare of achievement
yet nothing I do is ever good enough.

This is Lucifer
He is living in my breast

He tells me
I can have no life
No pleasure
No relationship.

Just when I think that I am safe
I hear his staccato heartbeat.

It says:
No good
Never
Not for you.

Now a woman comes
to help me claim my self.
She says:
Take the salt of the earth
and put it in his hair
it's a remedy so old
our mothers have forgotten it.

He says:
Be very careful
I do not work alone.
You know I have a wife
who looks a lot like you.

At this point, I was involved in a deadly collaboration with the negative masculine; I wanted approval so badly that I kept on listening to these devastating judgments. Such feelings of inadequacy are reinforced because our culture fails to honor feminine perceptions. While young women are encouraged to perform and to achieve, they find little support for their values and emotions. The authority figures in our society seem suddenly demonic because they rob a woman of her intrinsic worth.

A European fairy tale warns us of the consequences when a father fails to appreciate his daughter. It is called "The Handless Maiden." In this tale, a poor miller makes a bargain with the devil, and he unknowingly gives away his daughter for a pot of gold. The devil says simply, "If I make you rich, you must give me what is behind your barn." The miller agrees, thinking only of the apple tree, not knowing that his lovely daughter is also standing there. The devil comes to claim his prize, but he cannot touch the girl because she is too pure. In a rage, he insists that the father cut off both her hands and send her out into the world. Since the father is cowardly and fears for his own life, he brings this misery upon his child.

The young woman wanders along a country road, and after some time, she comes upon a palace garden. The king sees her and falls in love with her. He marries her and makes her a pair of silver hands. This seems to be a successful marriage, yet after a while the devil reappears, and our story takes another turn.

When the king is away, the young queen gives birth to a son named "Sorrowful." The devil sends a message to the king, informing him that the queen has been unfaithful. Then he forges a letter to the palace, commanding that she be put to death.

The queen escapes with her son and finds refuge in a nearby forest. She is taken care of by an angel, and she lives in a cottage with these words inscribed above the door: "Everyone may live freely here." In this place, the queen is healed and her hands are restored. One day the king rides into the wood in search of his family. He is perplexed when he discovers that the queen is not the helpless maiden he had known before. The queen then shows him the silver hands and explains that with god's help and nature's comfort, she was able to regrow her own. The family is now reunited, and the royal couple returns to the palace to celebrate the marriage once again.

In this tale, the trouble begins because the father does not understand the value of the feminine. He bargains with the devil and offers him an apple tree. Because apples were once sacred to the feminine, this act is bound to have grave consequences. Indeed, his only daughter loses her hands and also her basic hold on life. Today we continue to bargain away the rights of women and the earth and we, too, are in need of healing.

This fairy tale tells us that we must go outside the culture and ask the help of the heavens and the earth. We cannot be helped by man-made replacements or mechanical devices. We must work for deeper transformation. We must go into the forest to affirm our bond with nature and then listen to the angel who gives us the freedom to be as we are. Then, over time, we will we be able to grow back our hands and take hold of reality.

There is always something dangerous about the father-daughter relationship. When I was growing up, my father sent checks to Boys Town and tried to help some of the troubled young men in our community. I felt both challenged and humiliated by his actions. In response, I denied my femininity and tried to be the son he never had. I helped my father at his store and learned how to wield a baseball bat. Yet the physical closeness just wasn't there. I could not pit my strength against him like a son, and I was left with a deep sense of failure and inadequacy.

In those years, I turned to the Church for comfort, hoping for some affirmation of my way of being in the world. Yet what I found was another institution built upon the father-son relationship. I left the Sunday morning services with the feeling that I was not as "spiritual" as the men and my woman's soul was not as worthy of redemption. Now I felt rejected on two scores: my own father didn't love me, nor did the Father-God of Christianity.

For many years I felt guilty and ashamed of my femininity. I thought I was the only one to suffer such humiliation until I was in my thirties. Then I read *Fires,* a powerful critique of the patriarchy by Marguerite Yourcenar, which shows how this rejection took place in the life of Mary Magdalene.

In this version of the story, Mary is a chaste young woman preparing for her wedding night. The festivities are over and she waits for her bridegroom in a scented gown. When John comes to her room, he hesitates. He has joined a religious group that disapproves of the body and the senses. Marriage is allowed only to avoid the sin of fornication. "I represented the worst corporeal offense," Mary explains, "the legitimate sin approved by custom, so much more dangerous since it incurs no condemnation. [My groom] had chosen me, the most veiled of maidens, while secretly hoping not to succeed."

This woman is abandoned, not because her father made a bargain with the devil, but because her husband made a pact with God! John runs from his bridal bed to embrace the life of the spirit. And while he rises up, Mary begins her long descent. "A voice rising in the night called out for John three times, as it happens in front of houses where someone is going to die. John opened the window, leaned forward to gauge the shadow's depth and saw God. I saw only darkness."

This is the state of woman in the patriarchy; the son is welcomed, while the daughter is condemned to homelessness. Mary stumbles from her marriage bed and runs through the dark alleys of Jerusalem. She is raped by a Roman lieutenant, yet this violation of her body is nothing compared to the violation of her heart. She now believes John's assessment, that she has no value in and of herself, and so she gives herself to a Bedouin camel driver, an innkeeper, a sea captain, and a depraved philosopher. Slowly and deliberately she sacrifices any vestige of her former life.

At the end of the story, however, we see that Mary's wound is also her greatest strength. Since she gives herself to everyone, her life is free of self-concern and vanity. Though her body is rejected, her body is the vessel through which she is redeemed.

One day, in the marketplace, Mary finds herself kneeling at the feet of Christ. She is surprised that their lives bear a certain similarity: "He did not run from me. He bore the company of highwaymen, the contact of lepers, the insolence of policemen. Like me, he agreed to the terrible lot of belonging to all." In Mary and in Jesus, the many are made one.

Ours is the age of Mary Magdalene. We live out her story as we abandon the feminine and allow the earth to be raped and brutally destroyed. The only way we can change this situation is to confront our first experience of loss and rejection and begin to reclaim what is best and truest in ourselves.

When I tried to do this exercise, I was taken back to a summer I spent in the Greek islands. I had gone there after the publication of my first book to escape any criticism I might receive. Though I was a successful journalist, I was still plagued by that inner voice that said, "You're not good enough." I left my traveling companions behind one day and took a day sail to Naxos, to face my doubts and insecurities. On the way back, my boat was swamped and nearly capsized by a sudden storm. The other passengers crowded into the hull to escape the pitch and heeling of the heavy seas. Yet I crawled up to the high point on the ship and tied myself beneath the mast. As I lay there with my arms out to my sides, in the shape of a cross, I felt my body was the focal point for all the good and evil I had generated in this life. I became a kind of Manichaean map of the universe. In this moment, I felt the opposites pour through me, and I understood for the first time that there was no "worthy" or "unworthy," just this place within me that was made for the mixing of the light and dark. I began to weep; tears streamed down my face and mingled with the lashing of waves. I laughed and yelled at the storm as we moved into the harbor, the salt that once laced ancient ships now weighing and restraining me.

When I got into port, I walked up to the hill to find a taxi. I was so changed that Petrus, my usual driver, failed to recognize me. That night, I settled in my bungalow on a calm, protected beach. I dreamed that the earth had a large wound that kept breaking open, and I heard a voice say, "If you want to stop this wounding, you must be transformed."

It would take me nine years to finish this part of my journey. First, I had to strengthen my feminine side, which I did by spending time in nature and by creating my own rituals. I learned how to cast a protective circle, using stones and shells I had found in the woods near my home. One day I sat down in the middle of this circle and decided to confront the threatening male figure from my dreams. This man had appeared in many guises—a gangster, a prizefighter, a surly taxi driver. This time, he was a burly marine who tried to strangle me. I now began to talk to him in the hope that our relationship would finally begin to change:

I know you're not human; you are pure negative energy. But I want to know why you are trying to control me.

I am afraid you will overwhelm me with your power. That's why I attack.

What do you mean?

You women have been trapping me like this for centuries. I have not been known or respected for who I really am. When you get powerful and strong, you try to control and to manipulate. What do you think your incantations are about? You start with stones and rituals, and then you end up meddling with my powers.

I am beginning to understand. You feel that I am using you and manipulating you with magic. Yet I am trying to honor a feminine way of being in the world. Tell me, when was your spirit honored?

When men could use the energies of the night. To take the energy of the moon, you need a hunter's eyes. In those days, the moon was a masculine spirit. You had babies according to our phases; we also ruled the seas and the planting of the crops.

You have been cut out of our culture, the way so many women are today. Tell me, what happens if I give you back your share of the night? Do we have to go on fighting?

It will take a while for me to trust you. I am the masculine energy that has been here since eternity, but you have only been here for a single life!

You are the voice inside me saying, "You don't deserve to exist." In my dreams you murder me because you are afraid of feminine consciousness. You attack because you feel that you are vanishing! There must be some way to put an end to this.

Look at me. When we began this conversation, I projected myself as a tall, invincible marine. As you talk I am becoming softer and losing so much of my strength.

Yes, but now you are turning into a ray of moonlight. I can welcome you when you come to me in this guise. Whenever you are angry, I will remember that the masculine has been wounded, and I will try to offer you compassion. The female soul I carry has also been attacked. Perhaps we can be more careful with each other now. I see that you have been wandering this earth, looking for a place of entry into the human heart. Now that you have arrived, it is up to me to find out who and what you are. May I always have the courage to receive the Wounded Stranger as my guest.

Once I established a relationship with my dream figure, he was transformed from a cold killer to a nature spirit. In this exchange, I began to see how masculine energy grows destructive when it is cut off from the earth. When I had the strength to confront this figure and stop running from him, things really did start to change for the better. I saw that the world is full of wounded archetypes, and it is up to us to heal them and to humanize them.

After this dialogue, I was also able to understand my father. He had supported Boys Town because, at the age of fourteen, he, too, was homeless and a drifter. Though he later went to college and ran a business, he never forgot his harsh entry into manhood during the Depression years. He could not support me because, in his own life, he had yet to redeem the wounded masculine.

Over the years, the male figure in my dreams has appeared as a friend and guide and, with his help, I was able to reconcile myself with the Father-God of Christianity. I surprised myself one day by saying the prayer I had such great difficulty with so many years ago. It is a prayer of trust and abandonment that addresses our early sense of loss and reconnects us to the Holy Masculine:

> Father,
> I abandon myself into your hands;
> Do with me what you will.
> Whatever you may do, I thank you.
> I am ready for all,
> I accept all.

Let only your will be done in me,
and in your creatures.
I wish no more than this, O Lord.
Into your hands I commend my soul,
I offer it to you with all the love of my heart,
for I love you, Lord,
and so need to give myself,
to surrender into your hands
without reserve and with boundless confidence.
For you are my Father.

THREE

Toward a New Mythology

THE HERO AND THE HEART

*Who will not secretly rejoice when the hero puts his
armor off and gazes at his wife and son ... still
lovely and unfamiliar from the intensity of his
isolation and the waste of ages? Who will blame him
if he does homage to the beauty of the world?*

—Virginia Woolf
To the Lighthouse

WHEN I WAS A CHILD, I ACTED OUT MY FAVORITE myths and fairy tales. I was Beauty trying to heal the Beast in the middle of an enchanted forest or a lady locked in a high tower, awaiting rescue by a gallant knight who would bring me down to earth. While I considered the themes that had to do with marriage and with nature, the boys next door would set off on their own imaginary journeys; they would assemble armies and conquer distant territories. And in the process, they would slay dragons, enact new laws, and create new boundaries. The animating stories of our culture have to do with this kind of mastery, and for a while we have preferred these masculine tales of daring to the feminine tales of romance and relationship. Yet we have begun to ask, What story allows us to take part in the adventure and still be faithful to each other and to the beauty of the world?

The outer-directed energy of the hero has guided most of our major cultural and technical accomplishments so far. In the heroic mode, we have overly centralized our governments and deprived local regions of their character and autonomy. We have trivialized the feminine by separating women from their spiritual traditions and by ignoring our relation to the earth, and we have reduced nature to a mere commodity. It is clear that the hero myth has run its course and it can serve us once again only if it undergoes a major process of revisioning.

The scholar Joseph Campbell tells us that the hero's journey is not intended merely as an extroverted story of adventure. Instead, it is an inner quest. In his many battles, the hero conquers his longing for the safe and perfect world that was once provided by the family. What he wins is more than fame and immortality—it is an experience of life itself.

At some point in Western culture we lost touch with the inner values and began to see the journey differently. As far as I can tell, there was a major shift in our mythology around the sixth century B.C. At this time, the stories of Herakles and Theseus were doctored to favor a new political regime; in the revised versions, these two supermen go off to conquer neighboring lands. They take on the qualities of local heroes and absorb their popularity. In the process, they win the loyalty of the people and bind these outlying regions to a central government. To carry out its plan of expansion, Athens had to discredit the feminine nature cults as well. It would be hard to take over groves and rivers that were considered holy, and so main myths were "reinterpreted" to glorify the body politic over and above the body of the land.

Eva Keuls, the first scholar to look at Periclean Athens from a feminist point of view, calls this period the "Reign of the Phallus" and says it was based on a profound cultural imbalance. "[In this] society men sequester their wives and daughters, denigrate the female role in reproduction, erect monuments to the male genitalia, have sex with the sons of their peers, sponsor public whorehouses, create a mythology of rape, and engage in rampant saber-rattling. . . . In other cultures, generally dominated by men, much of their art and ritual presents the phallus as a symbol of generativity and of union with the female. [In Athens, however, we see] the display of the phallus as . . . a kind of weapon: a spear or war club and a scepter of sovereignty."

This ideal of masculine supremacy was all-pervasive. In the major plays and legends of the time, for example, it is the father who delivers life:

It is not the mother who is the parent of the child
although she is so called; she is merely nursemaid
to the newly planted fetus. He who mounts is the
one who gives birth; she, a stranger to a stranger,
merely preserves the seed if god does not destroy it.
And I'll give you proof of my argument: there can
be fatherhood without a mother. (Eumenides [658–
63], *Aeschylus,* Apollo speaking)

In the best-known myth of male fertility, Zeus gives birth by
himself, producing Dionysus from his thigh and Athene from
his head. Keuls relates, "Athenian motifs consist of tales of goddesses who could not or would not bear children and of stories
of male motherhood, in which offspring are born from parts of
the male anatomy or directly from male semen." This new belief gave Athens the grounds to deprive women of their rights
and property and to ban their most important holidays.

The only celebration remaining was the Adonia that focused
on the handsome young Adonis and his lover, Aphrodite.
Adonis was a "soft male" who aligned himself with women,
and as such, he was bound to be unpopular with the men of
Athenian society. Says Keuls, "The figure of the kind, even
timid, young lover in the Classical Greek context was a coun-
tercultural symbol, the antipode of the male model canonized
by society and embodied by Herakles and Theseus, brawny,
aggressive strong-men." Among the upper classes, men showed
little interest in family life, and during the festival of the ideal
lovers, Athenian women were especially mindful of their diminished state. One spring, they left their houses before dawn and
cut off all the phalluses on the public statues. This symbolic
castration puzzled scholars for many years until Eva Keuls
linked it to an early women's protest movement.

At no time in history were the sexes more polarized. This
marital alienation was reflected in the new mythology, especially in the life of Herakles. In the beginning, Zeus and Hera
are at war, and the divine marriage isn't working. Our robust
hero is a bastard, a product of Zeus' prodigality, and Hera tries

to kill the child. First, she sends two snakes into his cradle, but the brawny babe strangles them with his bare hands. Then she imposes a series of twelve labors that pit the hero against a whole range of deadly creatures. In this dragon-fight mythology, the hero confronts the darker powers of the feminine and takes a stand against the natural world.

However, Joseph Campbell reminds us that the name *Herakles* originally meant "to the glory of Hera." In the first version of the story, we learn about the bond of love between the hero and the goddess. The snakes Hera sends to the hero's cradle are not instruments of death but instruments of initiation. (When a priestess was bitten by a snake, she received the gifts of wisdom and of prophecy.) Once we know this, the twelve labors take on a different meaning. The bloodshed becomes a religious sacrifice; animals are slain, not in wanton devastation, but in a ritual way that honors our connection to earth.

Herakles kills the Nemean lion and then takes on its attributes of loyalty and strength. He slays the hundred-headed hydra and the wild boar, two creatures that bring violence and destruction to the land. He saves the golden hind that was sacred to the goddess Artemis. He drives off a flock of iron birds that are ravaging the fields. Herakles even takes over general housekeeping tasks, cleaning out the Augean stables, which have not been touched for centuries. Later he searches for the Cretan Bull that was loved by Queen Pasiphae and rounds up the man-eating mares. He retrieves the girdle of the Amazons and recovers the lost cattle of his friend, Geryon. In the process, he exacts tributes from many lands and rearranges many boundaries. In these labors, we see a dialogue between man and nature. Nature is subdued but not diminished. Feminine appetites are regulated but not denied. Masculine order prevails, yet the earth continues to challenge this regime with her natural creativity.

In his final labors, Herakles must find the golden apples of the West that were given to Hera as a wedding gift. These apples are sacred, and they symbolize the miracle of birth. Next,

Herakles is initiated into the Eleusinian mysteries that are all about the regeneration of the earth. The hero's journey now appears to be one long prelude to relationship and its theme, the constant balancing of male and female energies. Our question now is this: How can we reclaim this vision of the world?

I don't want men to stop being heroes. I like their courage and daring, their ability to risk and triumph over danger and adversity. Yet I am also drawn to the man who cares about home and family and gives some thought to the preservation of the world. Virginia Woolf felt the need for this kind of male emancipation in the 1920s: "How can we alter the crest and spur of the fighting cock?" she asked. "So many of the young men, could they get prestige and admiration, would develop what is now so stunted—I mean the life of natural happiness."

Men need to make this transition from action and adventure to the realm of feeling and relationship. This is something they must do, not just for the women in their lives, but for the sake of their own wholeness and integrity. What happens if they stay stuck in their youthful striving and ambition? We have only to consider the fate of Theseus, the second most popular hero of the Greeks.

Every year a group of fine young men and women from Athens must be sent to the king of Crete to be sacrificed to the Bull God. The representatives are usually selected by a lottery, but Theseus, prince of Athens, boldly volunteers, hoping he can find a way to save the delegation. This is a tale of daring and adventure—yet the outcome is not dependent on Theseus alone. As soon as he disembarks from his ship, he arouses the love of the Cretan princess Ariadne. This impetuous girl decides to help him. First, she tells him about the minotaur, a monster that is half man, half bull, and that lives in a labyrinth beneath the palace floor. Ariadne shows him how to reach the minotaur at the center of the maze and supplies him with a golden thread to find his way back out again. Theseus quickly slays the creature, frees his comrades, and sets sail for Athens, taking Ariadne. On their journey home, however, he carelessly abandons the princess on the windswept isle of Naxos where the dark god Dionysus claims her as his bride.

This is the story of two young people who live according to their separate passions: Theseus is on a quest for adventure and Ariadne on a quest for love. All of this seems natural enough, yet from the beginning, we are in a tragic mode. This young, idealistic woman must be abandoned by her lover, for he is committed to greater passion—the mastery of the world on his own terms. Ariadne's gifts are not respected though she is beautiful and wise. The story simply tells us that there is no room for the feminine at the center of the hero's life.

Our story also goes on to illustrate how the entire culture suffers from a young man's vanity and ambition. Theseus heads for Athens so full of his own exploits that he forgets a promise he made to his father. If his mission succeeded, he would change his sails from black to red. When his father sees the dark sails entering the harbor, he assumes that Theseus is dead. In his grief, he throws himself into the sea.

In myths, such things do not happen accidentally. The hero brings death to those around him because he puts his own achievements over human feeling. For centuries, men have been taught to ignore their natural affections as they enter the heroic realm. In the process, our relationships are damaged, and we end up with a society based on rank and power, not on a respect for life.

In the magazine *Changing Men*, Daniel Cohen asks us to rethink the myth of Theseus so it reflects the necessary balance between inner and outer values:

> This is what they do not tell us. They do not tell us
> that as Theseus entered the labyrinth, he was afraid

but refused to acknowledge his fear. They do not tell us that as Theseus heard the minotaur's bellows, he realized that they were songs, sometimes so sad that he wanted to cry, but he suppressed his feelings and marched on. They do not tell us that when he met the minotaur, he saw the beast-man had his own features. They do not tell us he was so enraged by this that he instantly killed the minotaur. They do not tell us that, confident nothing of the animal remained in him, he went on to rape many women, calling it love, and to kill many people, calling it glory.

In the new version, Theseus will enter the labyrinth in service of the Lady Ariadne. He will make his descent into the unconscious where all relationships are born. He will enter the maze afraid of the minotaur's cries but hopeful he can mend the situation. At the heart of the labyrinth he will find a creature who looks just like him. He will joyfully embrace his brother and they will dance and sing together. He will return the thread to Ariadne and she will weave a tapestry to celebrate the marriage of the ordinary world and the mysteries of the labyrinth. And then he will wait for the minotaur to seek him out again.

In this retelling of the myth, the hero moves beyond the realm of power and aggression. As he embraces the minotaur, he redeems his own lost feelings and emotions. He begins to understand that compassion is neither shameful nor unmanly. Indeed, it is the key to relationship and his connection with the living world. A man might meet the minotaur today as he confronts the possible breakup of his marriage or considers how his profession harms or alters the environment. The minotaur will bring a crisis of conscience and force him to ask, How do I honor my connection with the feminine? Am I really committed to my loved ones and to the preservation of the earth? The answer will come only when we have the courage to put aside our old defenses and go into the labyrinth unarmed.

————————— ❀ —————————

There are other stories in Greek mythology that show us how to move toward reconciliation. We have only to consider the return of Odysseus at the end of his long sea journey. When he embraces his wife, Penelope, the years of bloodshed and of battle are redeemed, and he makes his peace with nature and the feminine. In Book XI of *The Odyssey*, Tiresias, the seer, tells our hero how to prepare for this reunion:

> Go overland on foot, and take an oar,
> until one day you come where men have . . .
> never known the sea
> nor seen seagoing ships, with crimson bows . . .
> The spot will soon be plain to you, and I
> can tell you how: some passerby will say,
> "What winnowing fan is that upon your shoulder?"
> Halt, and implant your smooth oar in the turf
> and make fair sacrifice to Lord Poseidon:
> a ram, a bull, a great buck boar; turn back,
> and carry out pure hecatombs at home
> to all wide heaven's lords, the undying gods,
> to each in order. Then a seaborne death
> soft as . . . mist will come upon you
> when you are wearied out with rich old age.

In the first half of his life, the hero learns by doing, by applying his own energy to the cause at hand. Then there comes a time for inward turning. At this point, he must find a place where his fame is unknown, make a sacrifice to the feminine (hekatombs were offerings to the goddess Hera), and celebrate the virtues of the home.

In midlife, men and women come together and honor one another in a different way. By then, we have each played our separate roles and learned to forge our own identities. This is the moment when the hero looks with pleasure on his wife and child. He returns from his day's adventure, not as the ogre or the tyrant, but as the loving spouse. And all the battles are won because the hero finally *knows himself.* Some years ago, I wrote the following poem, "Odysseus Returning," to show what happens when we move beyond the quest for mastery and power and learn to look with awe and wonder at the world:

I have come home
but this is not the place that I expected!
I move now
in open spaces
break
faster than the light
All things come and wander through me
and my body is the anchor
for the pitch and heeling of the heavy seas.
To lie here once
is to be alive through all the journeying.

We rush so quickly through the first half of life that we rarely have the time to enjoy it. Youth is spent in an extroverted frenzy of achievement: the mad dash to the train, the harried hours at the office, the competition for the bigger mortgage and the better job. By middle age, we no longer want to hear the siren's call or yield to the old intensity and excitement. We are ready to stop and savor what we have, to open to the magic of the ordinary. Roger Rosenblatt describes this transformation of the hero in his essay "Captain Midlife":

Captain Midlife has never got it into his thick, frangible skull that his life is exactly where it is, consisting of a loving wife, three loving children, and a loving dog. . . . Well, sometimes he understands this, and sometimes he does not. When he does not, his mind packs up its belongings and sets sail like Ulysses (the very first Captain Midlife), hopping from port to port, dreaming up a storm. The Captain knows too well what the voyage of Ulysses was

all about. Circe gives the old come-hither. Calypso
does her little dance. The Sirens sing. No need to
tie the buzzard to the mast. He's been tied there all
along. *The Odyssey:* one long wild fling. But in
reality, the Captain stays close to shore these days,
and there he often amazes himself by falling in love
with his actual surroundings. Middle age expands
one's range of loving. The objects of his deepest affection are things he once ignored or took for
granted.

Such as his house. Suddenly the Captain finds
that he cares strongly for tables, doorknobs, chests
of drawers. . . . Friends, too, he loves, the older the
friends the dearer. . . . One day when he is old
enough, Captain Midlife may call a convention of
his words, spread them on the floor before him and
write an autobiography. It would begin with a description of the Captain as a boy, when he lived beside a park into whose thicket of dark trees he
would peer at night . . . and search for the love who
awaited him there. . . . Off they would fly together,
eventually to marry. After awhile he would leave
her to test new waters, and she would write her life
upon a loom.

In the end, the Captain would return, as all Cap-
tains do, to the girl of his dreams.

This is the universal story of the hero: youth is a time for
exploration, for trials both real and imaginary. Yet there must
also be a homecoming, a time to remember what the journey
has been *for.* At this point, the hero discovers the life of natural
happiness; he feels a new connection to the home and to the
hearth. As Rosenblatt says, the Captain returns to the girl of
his dreams. In truth, the girl has never left him; this is the inner
feminine who speaks to us of the beauty of the world and calls
on us to reconcile the hero and the heart.

Men are not the only ones who need to transform their heroic energy. Women also get caught up in the world of high

performance, and many of them fall into the trap of trying to be "one of the boys." The story of Atalanta is valuable here, for it shows how this kind of woman confronts the challenge of relationship in the second half of life.

Atalanta had a tough beginning. Because she was born female, her father left her on a lonely mountainside to die. She was suckled by a bear and raised by a group of hunters in the rugged forests of Arcadia, and grew up to be an outstanding athlete. As strong and swift as a man, Atalanta defeated the great wrestler Peleus at the Olympic Games and also sailed to find the Golden Fleece. While she won many trophies, the Delphic Oracle urged her not to marry, citing her disregard for woman's ways.

Atalanta's most famous deed was the stalking of a giant boar that destroyed the Calydonian countryside. Atalanta's spear stopped the animal as it charged; then the young Prince Meleager went in to complete the kill. When the hunt was over, he offered her the boar skin as a trophy and asked her to be his wife. Meleager's mother was incensed, and in a fit of rage, she threw her son's protective amulet into the fire. He was struck dead as he lay his head on Atalanta's breast.

Atalanta and Meleager represent the first love of adolescence, a love that in ancient Greece was generally directed at a person of one's own sex. It is an attraction based, not on difference, but on a shared identity. (When Atalanta had a child from this alliance, she did not know what to do with it. Some say she abandoned it because she had no contact with her mother or with the goddess of childbirth.)

Atalanta's athletic feats won her many honors, and one day she was reunited with her father. All went smoothly until he began to pressure her to marry and start a family of her own. Atalanta replied that she would wed the man who could beat her in a footrace, knowing this was an impossible task.

One day, a youth named Hippomenes fell in love with Atalanta and asked Aphrodite for her aid. The goddess was intrigued by this young woman who put so little stock in her beauty and attractiveness and she gave this suitor three golden apples from the garden of the Hesperides. These apples were sacred to all women and would prove invaluable in beating Atalanta at her own game. During the race, Hippomenes rolled the golden apples at her feet. Unable to resist them, Atalanta stopped and picked them up, and the young man beat her to the finish line. All did not end well, however, for the couple ran off to consummate their marriage without honoring Aphrodite. In revenge, the goddess turned them into lions and made them draw her chariot across the sky.

In our present culture, it is very common for a young woman to live like Atalanta in the first half of life. Such a woman is usually a "father's daughter." Her model of initiation is male, her mentors are male, her mode of behavior is forthright and aggressive. An Atalanta woman usually takes marriage far too lightly. She embarks on this relationship thinking that it is just one more adventure. She accepts the golden apples, but does not understand their deeper meaning. The apples do not belong to the masculine world of action but to the feminine realm of opening and receiving. Indeed, they embody a woman's ability to nourish and sustain new life. The apple itself is called "the love fruit," and when it is cut open, it resembles the womb. The trouble is that the golden apples have been missing from our culture for a very long time.

Since Atalanta's day, we have judged ourselves by masculine standards of accomplishment and forgotten about our feminine values. At times, even the women's movement has failed to recognize the importance of feeling and relationship. In the past, we have fought for better jobs and equal pay but not for a way of life that would also allow the time we need to cherish our families and our friends.

Like Atalanta, I was raised to be successful in a world of men, and I have also found it hard to move from the battles of the day into the more feminine realm of family and relationship. When I was in my twenties, I was married to a publishing executive who came home from the office, wanting to talk

about the different aspects of his work. I responded with heroic
zeal, telling him how to manage his staff, run his department,
never realizing that he simply needed to be honored and appre-
ciated. Like Atalanta, I was so intoxicated with my own ambition that I did not know how to listen to his account with
patience and with love.

When an Atalanta woman marries, she will usually pride
herself on being an "efficient" wife. She fails to realize that love
is not a matter of performance and that relationship requires a
different sensibility. Atalanta may even think of motherhood in
the heroic mode and see it as a thing to be prepared for like a
race. I wrote this poem several years ago, convinced that Atalanta married to achieve another kind of glory. In this version,
she weds to produce a group of strong-limbed daughters who
will duplicate her best accomplishments and pose a challenge
to the gods.

What else could I grow up to be?
Suckled by a bear,
and raised by a bunch of lonely hunters
          in the forests of Arcadia.
What was I supposed to do?
Cook fancy dinners round a small wood fire?
Embroider geometric patterns on hides
          that kept us warm in winter lairs?

These days you only hear about the flashy stuff.
How I nearly strangled Peleus,
          wrestling at the games,
that boar I slew in Calydonia,
or the time I had convincing Jason
I could pull the sheets on the good ship Argos
with his raucous crew.

After all this hard-won glory,
          why give it up for any man?
I'll tell you, so you don't think I was taken
          by some untried youth,
when the brave Achilles might have had me
          for his bride.

And so you don't think I was hoodwinked
        by some golden apples,
filched from the Hesperides
and from Aphrodite's pride.

The truth is I got tired of all that running around
and of boasting with the boys.
Sure, I could have taken all my suitors,
        but I had other things in mind.
Who else could create a finer group of
        strong-limbed daughters
unless that virgin, Artemis, would try?

Well, you know how the story goes.
The crowd was angry
        and claimed I'd thrown an easy victory.
But think, how furious would Aphrodite be
if she knew my plans were more ambitious
than to seduce her poor Hippomenes?

In this tale of vanity and self-love, Atalanta marries, not because she cares about her husband, but because she wants to live on through her children. From the start, her goal is fame, and she offers no apologies.

For an Atalanta woman to have a real relationship, she must overcome her addiction to achievement and begin to understand that performance is not the only goal in life. This kind of realization usually hits some time around midlife. By then, Atalanta's competitive energy has simply run its course, and it is time for reassessment. I experienced this transformation several years ago when I worked in women's sports. My colleagues put on women-only races in twenty-five countries, while I wrote articles on the psychology of running and lobbied to get the women's marathon included in the Olympic Games. Atalanta was pictured on the medals we gave out to every race participant. In general, Atalanta had a positive effect, encouraging women to be more self-confident. Yet her negative side came out in the women like me who worked behind the scenes. Routinely logging sixteen-hour days, we lived out Atalanta's obsession with endurance. Without realizing it, we sacrificed our personal lives to serve a cause. Years later, a co-worker wrote: "I worked so hard to advance women's running but my marriage was a humiliating failure. I was so caught up in women's sports that I had nothing left over for my husband or myself."

We were each so involved in our own heroic efforts that we lost touch with our need for relationship. When the group disbanded, we each had to learn from Atalanta's errors and try to shift our energies. Our challenge was also to learn how to enjoy ourselves and live in a less driven way. When I found myself involved in another demanding project, putting in long hours on a magazine, I had a warning dream: I was typing a memorandum, and I kept misspelling the word *perfection*. It was too much of an effort, and no matter how I tried, I couldn't get it right.

In her struggle to achieve, a modern-day Atalanta kills a part of her psyche. She is simply too busy *doing* to take the time *to feel*. A whole generation of young women has now been trained to compete and to drive themselves this way. On the positive side, such women tend to be self-motivated and highly idealistic. They are skilled and accomplished, and they have an innate sense of what is fair and right. Yet to reach this level of achievement, their personal needs are often sacrificed. This kind of woman may try to change the world, but she also has another task, and that is to redeem her inner life. At some point, Atalanta must find her own values and stop living for the cheering of the crowd.

In the course of my research, I discovered an ancient text on alchemy that views Atalanta as a symbol of growth and transformation. For this group of initiates, Atalanta represents the struggle to unify the opposites, to bring together masculine and feminine polarities. In our story, the golden apples magically facilitate this union, but in real life this kind of reconciliation requires a long period of apprenticeship. The alchemists knew this and dedicated their entire lives to the quest for inner harmony.

The modern woman is called to finish Atalanta's journey and to work toward her own sense of wholeness and completion. If she starts out on the heroic path, she will develop a good sense of her own strengths and capabilities. Once she learns how to be tough and disciplined, she must also learn how to open to the energies of love. After "conquering the world," she must surrender to relationship and honor her own inner life. This is the balance we all must achieve if we wish to create a better ending for ourselves.

What happens when a woman's desire to love is overshadowed by her heroic need to win? She harms the earth and proves as violent and destructive as the men. When the great hero Achilles meets Penthisilea, the Queen of the Amazons, we see how this tragedy unfolds.

In the original version of this story, Achilles slays Penthisilea and rapes her corpse upon the battlefield. Yet the nineteenth-century German playwright Heinrich von Kleist gives us a new twist that illuminates "fighting female energy."

At the beginning of our tale, Penthisilea receives a delegation of soldiers who ask for her aid against the Trojans. In their company is the fair Achilles. To impress him, this eager queen prepares a charge against both sides. Her recklessness and daring are but attempts to win his praise, and her war dance is a form of courtship unlike any he has ever seen. Achilles is taken by her beauty, and in the final skirmish he rushes in to fight her, hand-to-hand.

To his surprise, Achilles is overcome and taken prisoner by the wild-haired queen. Then, in the Amazon camp, he is decked with flowers and prepared for the sacred marriage rites. The women are about to lead their captives in the Feast of Roses, a ceremony of lovemaking that is necessary to renew their tribe.

There is genuine feeling between the Amazon who is a force of nature and the hero who is exalted by the state. The trouble is that neither party knows how to behave; both the Amazon and the hero have moved beyond the limits of their culture, and their old traditions do not apply.

Though Penthisilea has won Achilles fairly, he begs her to return him to his regiment. She does so out of compassion for her lover, but the high priestess reminds her of her obligation to uphold the marriage rites. Penthisilea decides to attack again, then inaugurate the Feast of Roses with the brave Achilles at her side. She is desperate for victory as she calls the fiery women to her aid:

> Come then you victory crowned virgins, come
> You daughters of Mars, from head to foot
>   still thick
> Encrusted with the blood-caked dust of battle,
> Come, leading each by the hand that Argive youth
> That she has vanquished on the field of war. . . .
> How may I celebrate a festival
> More heavenly than heaven's own joyous pomps—
> The wedding-feast of the dread brides of war.

Penthisilea is wounded in this new raid, and while she is recovering, Achilles suggests that they meet again in hand-to-hand combat. The queen is horrified because she knows such an engagement can only lead to her humiliation and defeat. Achilles, on the other hand, is pleased with himself for having come up with such a practical solution. He proposes that the victor of this skirmish win the right to be married according to the customs of his land. Since the queen is ailing, he hopes things can be settled fast. Then he can take her back to Athens as he would a more conventional bride.

Penthisilea is not operating on this objective level, however. She is furious to find that her love is met with nothing more than rules and strategies. And she is enraged that Achilles would take advantage of her injuries. Here we see the difference between masculine and feminine aggression: Penthisilea fights to express her deepest feelings, and Achilles fights for what he thinks is fair and just. In the end, it makes no difference that the war is fought for love.

Penthisilea's wrath proves to be the strongest. In a fit of rage, she attacks Achilles and sends her shaft into his throat:

> He, writhing in a pool of his own gore,
> Touches her delicate cheek and calls to her:
> "Penthisilea! What doest thou? My beloved!
> Is this the Feast of Roses thou didst promise?

By now, the Amazon is in such a state that she cannot even hear her lover's voice; so she sets at him with her dogs. She tears his limbs from his body and then turns her fury on the landscape. The women disavow her awful deed and look in horror on their ailing queen:

> Oh, dreary waste,
> Barren as desert sands where no grass grows!
> Gay gardens which the lava flow has wasted.
> Seethed in the earth's dark womb and belched afar
> O'er all the blossoming paradise of her heart—

The world is indeed dark when Penthisilea awakens from her trance. At first she does not believe she is responsible for her lover's death:

> So—it was a mistake—kissing, biting—
> Where is the difference? When we truly love
> It's easy to do one when we mean the other. . . .

These are only ravings; when she realizes what she has done to her lover and to the rose-decked countryside, she picks up her dagger and aims it at her heart.

A woman who lives in the heroic mode has great skill at wounding; yet her greatest weapon is not her sword but her *emotion*. The queen destroys Achilles with an *excess* of feeling because she feels her love has not been accepted and received. What a union this would have been between the Queen of the Amazons and the greatest hero of all time. Yet what an impossible thing it is to achieve! The lovers too easily fall back into the quest for dominance and power. The hero takes refuge in games, while the Amazon is driven to a frenzy because her trust has been betrayed. Both are skilled warriors, willing to give themselves in battle. But they fail to understand that love demands another kind of sacrifice. In relationship, we cannot be concerned with winning; instead, we must have the strength *to be*—to bear up in those moments when we do not feel accepted. Love asks us to put down our armor and offer ourselves up, knowing all the while that there are no guarantees.

In this story we are reaching for a new and different way of being. The Amazon represents the ruthlessness of nature and the untamed energies of life. The hero represents a culture that tries to control our passion and our instincts. Yet we kill the possibility of relationship when we go too far in either direction. Until we reach a point of inner balance, we must put down our weapons and pray that a new solution can be found. It is easy for us to fall into this deadly competition—in which we try to prove which sex is more skilled and competent. This has been the downfall of so many modern marriages. A couple may begin with mutual respect and admiration but end up engaged in a brutal contest of the wills. Eros is destroyed when men and women are so consumed with strategizing and with the heroic need "to win."

Over the years, I have dreamed about Penthisilea and the golden armor of the Amazons. I have admired her strength and daring, but she has always made me wary of my own capacity for violence toward the masculine. From Penthisilea, I have learned that a woman is dangerous to others when she feels her creativity blocked and she is not allowed to love.

When a myth is told from a woman's point of view, the emphasis is on our ability to merge with others and identify with the creative powers of the earth. I have begun to see that there is a danger in this: A woman needs some masculine objectivity and detachment if she is not to confuse the goals of nature with her own personal and private ends. This is what Penthisilea does when she cannot have Achilles; she indicts him for a crime against nature when her passion is rejected. In the end, she destroys the man she loves and brings dishonor to her tribe.

When this myth is told from a man's point of view, the focus is on our separation from nature and from the Mother image. The danger here is one of alienation: Like Achilles, we may begin to trivialize the feminine, and then all relationship degenerates into a game of skill. If we are not to repeat this tragedy, we need a new set of stories to inspire us. These new tales can be neither matricentric nor patricentric. Instead, they must help us to find a new way of relating to one another and to the living world.

MARRIAGE AND THE RENEWAL OF THE WORLD

Let my marriage be brought to the ground. Let my love for this woman enrich the earth. What is its happiness but preparing its place? What is its monument but a rich field?

—Wendell Berry
The Country of Marriage

As I explore the relationship of man, woman, and nature, I find myself confronted with a strange and wondrous reciprocity. The earth depends for its renewal on our capacity for intimacy and union. In the same way I receive the beloved, I embrace the spirit that inhabits mountains, lakes, and trees. The fullness of one embrace nourishes and sustains the other, and together they make up the web of life. This is the ideal of the sacred marriage that can be found in many different cultures and philosophies. In this state, men and women no longer compete for power or control; instead, they honor one another and serve as loving stewards of the land.

This relationship was of great importance to early agricultural communities. At the beginning of the growing season, men and women would lie together in the fields and align themselves with the generative powers of the earth. In *The Golden Bough*, Sir James Frazer tells us that remnants of this ceremony survived well into the nineteenth century. In Western Europe, the mountain people chose a Green Man to be the husband of the earth. In Hildesheim, a young man was dressed in birch twigs so that nothing could be seen of him but his feet. He was known as the Leaf King. In Denmark, it was the custom to dress two small children as a bride and groom; adorned with flowers, they walked through the countryside and gave their blessings to the land. The maypole is also a relic of this ancient rite; it is a totem created by men and women of marriageable age, and with the interweaving of the ribbons, young people celebrate the dance of life.

In the Tarot deck, a set of divinatory cards that originated in the fourteenth century, we find the holy couple once again. This time the bride appears as the Queen of Disks. She is shown against a background of lush vegetation, symbolizing the fertility of the earth. Her consort cares for the animals and the crops. If we lose touch with these inner figures, the Tarot warns, "reason will be divorced from reality" and we will find ourselves "in a world gone mad with a riot of soulless mechanism." The sacred couple in the Tarot remind us that we are all a part of nature, that we must take on the burden of renewal of our own accord.

The idea of the sacred marriage also appears as a main theme in the tales of King Arthur and his Court. These stories serve as a reminder that we owe our allegiance, not just to the ordered hierarchies of the church and state, but to the spontaneity of nature. They represent the road not taken in Western mythology. While most of our stories focus on separation from the feminine and from the living world, the Arthurian romance emphasizes reconciliation. Here we see the meeting of nature and culture and an equal balancing of male and female powers.

The story that has long been my favorite is that of Dame Ragnell. Ragnell is an ugly damsel who appears at Arthur's Court to challenge its one-sided ideals of rationality and refinement. A creature of the wilds, Ragnell carries many of our negative projections. She is everything in nature that we deem unclean and unsafe. Yet she also teaches us how to redeem what is natural in ourselves.

On a hot midsummer's day, King Arthur rides into a dense and unfamiliar forest in pursuit of a beautiful white hart. In the excitement of the hunt, he begins to trespass on lands that do not belong to him. When he kills the hart, he is challenged by the owner of the forest, a dark and forbidding fellow named Sir Gromer Somer Jour. This dour stranger rides up to the king and angrily rebukes him: "Sire, you have taken a life within my forest. The penalty for this is death. But I will give you one more chance. I will spare your life if one year from now you can answer the following question: What is it that a woman wants more than anything in the world?"

Confident that he can find the answer by sheer reason, Arthur sends his pages out to question all the women in the land. Then he gathers together all this data and sets out to meet Sir Gromer Somer Jour. Along the way, however, he is approached by a hag with large warts on her chin, hard and leathery skin, and hair like a crow's nest, who is known as Dame Ragnell. She has the audacity to address him, saying, "Arthur. You do not have the proper answer. I alone have the information that you seek!"

The king wonders what wisdom could come from such a vile and uncultured creature. Yet Ragnell is persistent. "Think what you like," Ragnell says, "but when I am proven right, you must reward me. I want you to provide me with a husband. And I ask you for Gawain, the best and truest knight."

"Gawain is a free man," Arthur counters. "He is not mine to give away."

But Ragnell has a ready answer: "I only require you to tell Gawain of your situation and ask him to decide."

Feeling he has nothing to lose in such a bargain, Arthur agrees. Then he rides on to face the somber figure of Sir Gromer Somer Jour and begins to bargain for his life. At first, Arthur sits confidently on his horse as his pages read the several hundred answers they have prepared. But Gromer Somer Jour begins to grow impatient and starts to wave his axe high in the air. "I knew you would never solve this riddle!" he shouts. In desperation, Arthur blurts out the solution given to him by the ugly damsel. "What a woman wants more than anything is . . . sovereignty!"

"So you have found my sister!" says Somer Jour. "This could only be the work of Dame Ragnell."

Arthur now has no choice but to tell Gawain of his predicament. At this point, we find that Gawain is, indeed, a loyal knight for he offers to marry the ugly damsel right away. "No request can be too great," he replies, "if it would save your honor or your life."

Ragnell demands a full wedding ceremony—with everyone in the realm invited, the table set with silver and all the finest things to eat. She appears in her dirty dress and takes no pains to conceal her ugliness. Gawain beholds his bride with the warts on her face and cobwebs in her hair; he sees the wildness that cannot be tamed, the antithesis of the beauty and refinement that prevail at Arthur's Court. Yet, brave knight that he is, Gawain stands beside her and shows neither his fear nor his distaste.

The couple then retire to the bridal chamber where Ragnell demands to be received as any ordinary wife. Gawain hesitates and first gives her a light peck on the cheek. When he finally kisses her upon the lips, however, she turns into a beautiful young maid.

"I now stand before you in my true form," Ragnell explains. "My brother, Gromer Somer Jour, put a spell on me when I disagreed with the way he was disposing of our lands. Because I spoke my mind, he turned me into such a loathsome thing that no man would dare to look at me. He said I must remain that way until I wed the truest and the bravest knight.

"But the spell is not entirely broken," she tells the astonished groom. "You must make a choice: You can have me beautiful by day and ugly by night. Or you can have me ugly by day and beautiful at night. Which one will it be?"

For a long time Gawain is silent; after much thought, he says, "My Lady, I cannot determine such a thing. Since it is your life, you must decide."

With this, Ragnell rejoices: "The final condition was that my husband allow me to choose my fate. Now I am fully restored for you have granted me my sovereignty."

Ragnell is turned into a hag because she dares to contradict her brother and speak up about the condition of their lands.

Under patriarchy, women this direct and forthright are not treated kindly. They are considered "unattractive" and are generally referred to as "witches" and as "hags." This is how the inner feminine is treated today. No one wants to hear about our darker emotions or to confront our anger and our grief. And so this way of being is denied.

As this story opens, the men are trying to limit the expressive power of the feminine. Gromer Somer Jour casts a spell upon his sister, and it cannot be broken until she finds a man who is willing to grant her the autonomy she seeks. Somer Jour knows that few men will willingly entertain the hag, so he makes Ragnell as hideous as he can. Next, Arthur treats the damsel with contempt. To him, she is an embarrassment of nature and represents all the dirty and unpleasant things he does not wish to see. Though Ragnell gives him the answer that will save his life, Arthur turns his back on her because he does not value this dark, instinctive femininity. He then tries to solve the riddle in this story logically. And his inquiring pages come up with superficial answers that have to do with vanity and flattery—not with a woman's grounding in the natural world.

Later the king also tries to keep Ragnell from marrying Gawain. When she asks for the hand of "the bravest knight," Arthur reminds her that every man has the right of self-determination. This is an irony, for Ragnell does not have the ability to choose her destiny, and in this "well-intentioned" patriarchy the rights of women and the earth are frequently ignored.

How is reconciliation finally achieved? Not by Arthur, who represents the older generation, but by the young knight who has the strength to receive the very qualities the king finds so unpalatable and unrefined. Gawain has less fear of the feminine because he has already proven himself in the world of men. It is this self-knowledge that frees him to respond with grace and compassion. When Gawain makes love to Ragnell in the bridal chamber, he receives the figure that his culture fears the most. It was said that a hag could overpower even the strongest knight and rob him of his soul. Yet Gawain treats Ragnell with respect, and she is transformed into a lovely maiden.

At this point, however, Gawain must make another choice. Would he rather have his new bride beautiful by day—when all the court can see her and admire her? Or would he rather have her beautiful when they are alone in bed each night? The question itself is a trap. Should the knight answer either way, he would be answering basely, either because he is concerned with vanity and prestige or with the pleasures that he enjoys in private with his wife. Gawain's reply is wholly unselfish: "My Lady, since it is your life, it is up to you to decide." With this, he shows himself to be even wiser than the king. He has answered the riddle of the story, "What does a woman want most in all the world?" and he has done so with a trusting heart.

This story shows us that a happy marriage can be achieved only when the feminine and the earth are respected in their own right. Ragnell never fails to stand up for these values, even though to defend them, she often must appear in a less than flattering light. She appears before the king and the entire realm in her wild and unkempt state. She asks everyone to accept the darkness and unpredictability of nature and to allow all creatures to exist in their own right.

Jungian analyst Polly Young-Eisendrath says the hag plays an important role in couples therapy today. The hag is constellated when a woman feels she has to repress her feelings and when she realizes that the feminine is not honored in her marriage. Like King Arthur, many husbands want to solve the riddle of existence in a logical and ordered way. They are reluctant to embrace the irrational, to delve deeply into their emotions and confront the unknown in themselves or in their mates. Young-Eisendrath believes that most therapies support the underlying values of the patriarchy, and, therefore, we try to calm and anaesthetize the hag. If this is so, then it is no small thing for a woman to stand up like Ragnell and make her case so openly. But is there any choice? If we do not behave this forthrightly we will only make matters worse with our denial and dishonesty.

Many of us have been taught to repress our basic feelings and to deny our values in order to remain in a relationship. Yet that does both parties a disservice and leaves no room for growth. Unfortunately, our longing for "togetherness" is so dangerously addictive that it overshadows our true nature. We must remember that real relationship can happen only when men and women are in full possession of themselves. Ragnell teaches us about this kind of inner development: She knows what it is she wants, and then she asks for it, and there is no coyness or dissembling in this tale. She asks us to move beyond our concern for vanity and appearances and see that relationship is not about simply "being nice." Rather it involves a willingness to come into the field of conflict, to reveal those ugly and "unacceptable" feelings such as anger, fear, and loneliness. As Daniel Williams writes in *Spirit and the Forms of Love:*

> Love does not put everything at rest; it puts everything in motion. Love does not end all risks; it accepts every risk which is necessary for its work. Love does not resolve every conflict; it accepts conflict as the arena in which the work of love is to be done. Love does not separate the good people from the bad, bestowing endless bliss on one, and endless torment on the other. Love seeks the reconciliation of every life so that it may share with all the others.
>
> Love means to will the freedom of the other, the acceptance of the consequences of relationship to another, and the vulnerability which goes with that acceptance.

To keep things going smoothly day to day, we may need the etiquette of Arthur's Court, but we must not let it keep us from going down into the depths of life. We must risk being open to the hag and remember that relationship is not a neat and tidy thing. Instead, it begins and ends, as another Celtic poet said, "in the foul rag and bone shop" of the human heart.

This story addresses one of our deepest and most ancient fears. What happens if we grant the feminine its full autonomy?

Gromer Somer Jour is unwilling to take that risk. We find out why when we look more closely at his name. Gromer Somer Jour reminds us of the "Groom of a Summer's Day" who was sacrificed once a year to ensure the fertility of the crops. He is a throwback to an earlier era that believed in the ruthlessness of nature and the "bloodlust" of the land.

This tale of Dame Ragnell comes to us from the Middle Ages, and by this time, the feminine principle has been transformed. Gromer Somer Jour is about to kill the king to uphold the pagan custom of "paying back the earth," but Ragnell comes forward and stops the sacrifice. She saves the king because she needs his respect and cooperation. Ragnell knows that there must be a mutual honoring of masculine and feminine if we wish to renew the source of life.

I have learned a good deal from Ragnell's behavior. Throughout, she asks only to be seen for who and what she is. She is not devouring or controlling; instead, she is careful to offer others the autonomy she seeks. In the end, she is rewarded with a marriage based on real equality. Gawain proves to be her match, for he is an example of the conscious masculine. He does not wish to impose his will on others. Instead he respects the integrity of women and the earth. I believe the future depends on our ability to establish this kind of partnership.

To begin with, we must be more aware of our own inner ecology. Where are we strong and where are we dependent? When do we project our needs onto our mates? Gawain and Dame Ragnell provide us with a much-needed model: they show us that we must have a highly developed sense of self, if we wish to embark upon the sacred marriage and serve as loving stewards of the land.

"The Knight of the Lion" is a Celtic legend that teaches us how to distinguish between our many passions. First, it illuminates the love of adventure and accomplishment that we encounter in the blush of youth; then it illuminates the more seasoned love that comes from a profound respect for nature and the feminine. The first is really an infatuation with things that bolster and support the ego; the second asks us to identify with the larger purpose of the living world.

As this tale opens, the heroes of the round table are gathered around the fire, and Sir Calogrenant is bold enough to tell of his undoing. It is most unusual for a knight to speak of humiliation and defeat, and Calogrenant has dared to do so only because the king is sound asleep.

"It was Saint John's Day, at the summer solstice," he begins, "and I rode forth into a wondrous forest, filled with trees and blossoms. I met a yellow man who lives there with his daughter; everything in their house was gold, and the place was full of richness and delight. They asked me to remain with them, yet in the morning I put on my armor and set out on my quest. Soon I came upon a one-eyed giant who was hurling cattle down a mountainside. He was fierce and ugly, but I stood my ground with him. 'If you are not afraid,' he said, 'then I will let you pass. Ride through the forest of Broceliande, and you will find the Fountain of Life at the foot of a miraculous tree. This is the center of the world, and there you will have a great adventure.'

"I rode forth and found a fountain and a silver chalice beneath an extraordinary tree. I poured the waters on the stone, and all at once a terrible storm broke all around me, destroying the animals and the land. Then a knight in black armor came riding forth. 'You have unthinkingly harmed the earth and wounded my whole kingdom,' he said. 'Now you must pay for this!'

"He charged me many times, and I was finally overwhelmed by his greater skill and strength. Then he unseated me, and I had to make my way back home alone and humiliated, without my lance and steed. From that day on, I have never spoken of the Black Knight or of that fateful day when he defeated me."

The other knights are now eager to take up the challenge. "We'll set off tomorrow and restore the honor of Calogrenant!"

In the audience, there is a dark youth named Yvain who has yet to prove himself at Arthur's Court. He sets out early to challenge the Black Knight, and after an all-night journey, he finds the fountain. He steps forth and spills the waters of life. The sky darkens and a terrible storm sweeps across the earth, destroying every living creature in its path.

Moments later the Black Knight rides out to challenge him. Yvain lunges forward, and his lance pierces the helmet of the Black Knight, lodging deep within his brain. Mortally wounded, the Master of the Forest turns back toward the castle, unaware that he is followed by Yvain.

Once inside the fortress, the hero is championed by Lunete, a lady-in-waiting who gives him a magic ring. This ring makes him invisible so he can move freely about the castle and attend the funeral of the Black Knight. There Yvain falls in love with the Lady of the Fountain, the fairest woman he has ever seen.

The following day, Lunete urges the Lady to take another husband, for the forest is undefended and word has come that Arthur's men are about to challenge their domain.

"There is no man in the world skilled enough to take the place of the Black Knight!" the Lady mourns.

"Not true," says Lunete. "One man has challenged him and won, and I will bring him here."

At the urging of her council, the Lady of the Fountain consents to wed Yvain.

In the morning, Arthur's men spill the waters of life, and a new knight rides out to challenge them. When all the men have been unseated, Yvain takes off his helmet and tells of his adventure. After a great feast, a treaty is signed, and the men ask Yvain to return with them to Arthur's Court and take part in their games. The Lady of the Fountain knows the worth of her new husband; yet she allows him this temporary leave, asking only that he return next summer on the eve of Saint John's Day.

In Arthur's world, the time goes quickly. Autumn is spent in jousting; winter, in storytelling and in endless games of chess; spring, perfecting new games and outdoor exercises in the fresh, sweet air. Then summer comes, and a major tournament is held to mark the passing of Saint John's Day. One evening, a hooded figure rides up to the castle. Lunete has come to confront Yvain and to take his wedding ring away. "You have betrayed us," she accuses. "You have left the forest unprotected, and you have forgotten the promise you made to the Lady of the Fountain. This ring belongs, not to a boy, but to a man."

Yvain trembles and in blind panic runs into the forest, where he is overtaken by his grief. He tears at his clothes and flesh. He falls and cuts himself on rocks and has no food and no protection from the elements. An old hermit takes pity on him and offers him a crust of bread. "It is no use," Yvain explains. "My journey is over, and I have lost the things I dearly love." Wisely, the hermit reminds him, "You cannot lose what you have never won."

Later, Yvain is helped by a noblewoman who makes him a gift of a horse and armor. In time, he is fit to resume his quest— only now it will not be for glory and adventure but to understand the mystery of love.

Yvain rides into a new and different land and comes upon a raging battle between a dragon and the king of beasts. The lion is trapped in a crevice in the earth, and Yvain feels pity for the creature and slays the fire-breathing serpent. The lion is so grateful that he hunts with Yvain and lays down next to him, keeping watch at night. Yvain is now in touch with his instincts and with his own animal nature. And the lion also awakens in him a true compassion for other living things.

The knight and the king of beasts go on to the share many adventures. And after a while, Yvain begins to call himself the "Knight of the Lion" in honor of his loyal friend.

One day the pair set out to find the Lady of the Fountain. Again Yvain enters the lush valley and spills the waters beneath the tree of life. Again, a storm sweeps over him. But this time, no challenger appears on a black horse. Yvain looks up the path and sees only a slender form.

"Sire, I have no protector," says the graceful Lady of the Fountain. "My husband has left me, and my forest is unprotected. Please do not harm my lands."

"I am called the Knight of the Lion, and I have come to be your guardian," the stranger offers. Yet when he removes his helmet, the Lady sees that her new champion is Yvain.

At first, she is angry and feels she has been tricked. Yet Yvain soothes her, saying, "I am not the callow youth who first came into these woods. Now I will serve you faithfully as my lion friend serves me."

The Lady of the Fountain accepts his pledge, and this time, she insists that they never be parted. From now on, when Yvain travels, the Lady will go with him. And they will share both the solitude of the forest and the fellowship of Arthur's Court.

Yvain weds the Lady and dedicates himself to the Fountain of Life. The trouble is he fails to understand their deeper meaning. Eventually he loses his kingdom, and his wedding ring is taken from him. For a while he wanders aimlessly, with no real purpose to his life. To heal himself, Yvain must begin to reconstruct his personality, beginning at the level of the instincts. In the end, he must become the "Knight of the Lion," a man who respects his own animal nature and honors his connection with the earth.

In the course of events, the Lady also is transformed. At the beginning, she is like the ancient Goddess whose sole purpose is to renew the land. She has little sense of her own individuality, and so she is afraid to leave the safe haven of the forest and attend the festivities at Arthur's Court. By the end of the story, she has learned to trust the masculine and to appreciate the culture and accomplishments of men.

The Fountain and the Court are meaningful symbols that reflect our two different ways of being in the world. As the scholar Heinrich Zimmer says, the Fountain in the middle of the forest is "the feminine realm; it offers an esoteric initiation into the powers of creation." The Round Table, in turn, represents the community of men and "their common adventures, tournaments and festivals." This story speaks of our continual need to balance the inner and the outer life.

This integration is particularly difficult for us today because we are so much like the young Yvain. We start out full of ambition, armed with reason, and equipped with all the best technology. Yet we do not know how to find the hidden forest, how to honor the inner world of the imagination and the dream. It is all too easy for us to lose ourselves in planned activity and forget the comforts of nature and of solitude.

This story is about our search for a more balanced way of being in the world. That is the meaning of the silver chalice that Yvain finds at the entrance to the forest. This is none other than the Holy Grail, which enables us to reconcile the opposites. At first, Yvain does not know what to do with it; he carelessly spills the contents of this cup, and then the lands are devastated. The Jungian analyst Robert Johnson reminds us that it is not uncommon for a young man to make such a mistake when he first encounters the grail. The trouble is he does not know what to do with it, and nothing in his life so far has prepared him for this powerful experience. This is why Yvain so easily forgets the Lady of the Fountain when he returns to Arthur's Court. He puts aside his solitary encounter with nature and the feminine to engage in public games of skill and combat. Like Yvain, so many of us abandon our feelings and emotions and choose to live in a completely extroverted way. The chalice, however, is a symbol of our inner integration: it tells us that we have to heal this split within ourselves.

The grail quest is also an opportunity to heal the outer rift between men and women. The cup represents the love between the sexes that cannot be forced but must be freely given. In an older version of the tale, a king named Logres attacks the Lady of the Fountain and robs her of her silver cup. After its loss, women no longer trust the men, the trees are bare, the grass and flowers wither, and there is little life-giving water left upon the earth. The women then wait for a Desired Knight to renew this relationship and actively participate in the greening of the land.

Some years ago, I dreamed that my husband came up to me, carrying water in a beautifully decorated ceremonial cup. We drank from it with a profound sense of mutual honoring. I was so affected by this dream that I began to explore this image in my books on world mythology. Tribal people knew that water was necessary to ensure the fertility of the earth. The Egyptians spoke about a primeval ocean that gives birth to all things. The Greeks honored water because it was required for the germination of a seed. In ancient times, dreams about water were said to be about rebirth. Psychologists today say that water is connected to the deep unconscious and to the feminine side of the personality. To find these healing waters, we must learn to make a place for feeling and imagination in our daily lives.

That is not an easy thing to do in a society that values action more than it values inward turning. It is fortunate for us, however, that our dreams reflect the quest for wholeness that is embodied by the grail. If we pay attention to them, we will receive some valuable clues about the integration of reason and emotion, nature and spirit, masculine and feminine. By way of illustration I would like to show you how these age-old themes have appeared in mine:

Dream 1.

I am walking into an ancient town. There is a cathedral that is buried in the earth, yet the main altar is now exposed to the surrounding hillside. I am to find a husband there.

Dream 2.

I am in a building where a religious service is taking place. I sit outside in the lobby and listen to the people chant and sing. Then the rabbi—a smiling Buddha of a man—bursts out, skipping. He says, "Follow me." I skip with him through the great hall and up and down a stairway. Then we get to a place where the steps alternate: one goes up and the other goes down. I jump only on the top steps. But the rabbi says, "No! This is the meaning: You must go down before you can go up. Do not skip over anything." He will find me a good husband if I learn to do this right.

Dream 3.

I am with my husband in a hotel. He has an interview for a teaching job at Yale. I am choosing my clothes and rushing around to get things done, and I hope that I will have time to change the linens on the bed. I am always changing my rhythms to be with him because I fear that I will lose him! I am trying to please others and forget to pay attention to myself.

Dream 4.

I am in a hotel room with my husband. We are making love but are interrupted when two women come into the room. One starts making coffee. The other one walks over to us. She is very short, and her face comes up to my husband's waist. However, she looks him straight in the genitals and says, "I want to talk to you."

This woman is capable of standing up to masculine energy and of being honest and direct about the things she wants in a relationship. At first, I am afraid of her and wish that she would go away.

Dream 5.

I am with my husband, who has brought me a bottle of gold dust. It has one word written on the label: "Quest."

Dream 6.

My husband and I are living on a farm. An old wise couple work the land across from us. We get

up at dawn and watch them seeding their crops. We
are inspired by them and start to lay out our summer garden. After a short time, it is blooming. It
looks lush when it is finished, and we make love to
one another in the open fields.

These dreams, which occurred over a period of seven years,
are all concerned with the conscious integration of masculine
and feminine. In the first, I walk into a church, and to my
surprise, I find an altar that is open to the sky and the surrounding hillside. For the first time, I began to see beyond the
patriarchal notion of the Father-God and discover that my spirituality must also be grounded in the earth.

The second dream is also about this kind of reconciliation.
The rabbi's teaching, "You must go down before you can go
up," tells me that I must tend to my body, and to my emotions,
as well as to my more rational way of being in the world. I
must go down into the depths even though I would rather skip
over that discomfort. When the rabbi advises me to make the
descent, he seems to be saying that the "ups" and "downs" are
a part of all relationship. He will help me find a husband, but
first I must do my inner work.

In the third dream, I finally have a partner. I am trying so
hard to please him, however, that I lose touch with my own
internal rhythms. This dream shows me that I am still caught
in the collective. I want to please a man, so I put my needs
aside. We are all trained in this kind of self-abnegation and
asked to honor the demands of our jobs and institutions over
and above our own response to life.

The fourth dream is also a warning: it says I must stop hiding
my real feelings. I must learn to be like the woman who looks
up at my husband and says very directly, "I want to talk to
you." A relationship of equals requires this kind of straight-
forwardness and honesty. At first, I am embarrassed by the
other woman, who seems to be too pushy and aggressive. Yet I
know I need some of her courage and directness.

By the fifth dream, I have made progress, and have begun to affirm my own way of being in the world. Now that there is an atmosphere of mutual respect, I trust the responses of my partner. At this point, I am ready to embark upon my own grail quest. My husband gives me a bottle of gold dust, and this is a very important sign. In alchemy, gold is considered the most precious metal because it symbolizes the conscious union of masculine and feminine.

The challenge, of course, is to translate this ideal into day-to-day reality. At this point, I dream about the old wise couple who run the farm across the street. The woman and her husband plant a garden and are bound together by their labors in the earth. This dream is also about the seeding of a marriage. Like any growing thing, intimacy requires a period of incubation, a time to deepen silently and in the dark. Only later do we offer up those feelings that have taken root, and we enter the phase of revelation, of unveiling. We must learn to trust in these organic cycles—to accept the times for growing together and the times that must be spent apart.

Relationship is not lived out in the same intensity at every moment. Rather, it is built upon an alternating pattern of solitude and activity, of nourishing and going forth. The last dream asks me to put my faith in this organic process. It reminds me that once we each achieve a sense of inner balance, something happens in the outer world: The fields grow lush and green, and the trust between men and women is restored.

The Challenge of Relationship

———————— ❀ ————————

Love and communion require inverse polarities. Through the course of history, you identify with the earth and I with the sky: cosmologies and fertile myths are renewed in us.

—Danilo Dolci
Palpito

WHEN THINGS DON'T GO SO SMOOTHLY, I REmind myself that men and woman have two different ways of being in the world. It is as though we occupy two disparate landscapes, and the beauty that attracts one holds so little promise for the other. The great mythologies tell us that we are destined to live out two different life patterns: The male must separate from the mother and define himself against the force of nature; the female must merge with others and identify with the larger cycles of the natural world. What could be more difficult than to find a common ground?

Only recently have we begun to see that life itself is a process of merging and of separating, that we are required to move back and forth between these two polarities. In recent years, science has given us an overview of the creative process and shown us how both masculine and feminine values are embodied in the journey of the human seed. The sperm aggressively fights its way up the birth canal, and as it penetrates the egg, it gives up its own identity. In a flash, the sperm loses its tail and then discorporates. This is our first experience of union on the physical plane.

Next, the living being enters a whole new phase of separation. Its intelligence goes into differentiating from the mother in order to leave her body. Later, the child will view itself as separate from the mother, spiritually and psychologically. Throughout life, however, the individual will be drawn to situations and relationships that help it to recapture that first memory of "the one."

This pattern is the basic grammar of existence. A healthy individual is comfortable with the whole organic process. In the past, however, human cultures have tended to get stuck in only one part of the journey. The early matriarchies, for example, had no understanding of male creativity, and when the earth produced and the womb bore fruit, it was assumed that women were responsible for it all.

Our ancestors believed that women's menstrual blood both fertilized the earth and caused a child to grow. Therefore, birth and regeneration were considered the sole province of the female. The earliest creation stories from Vedic India to the Middle East speak of a feminine deity who constructed every living creature from clay. She was called "the Mother of the universe," and the entire earth seemed to run according to her cycles. The phases of the moon, in harmony with the menstrual period, determined the time of planting and of harvesting as well as all the major rituals and holidays.

The primary intelligence of the ancient world was grounded exclusively in the female body. The Greeks spoke of the *omphalos*, or hub of the universe, as the holy womb. Wives were worshiped as divinities, and altars to the Goddess were placed at the entrances to every house. In Rome, temples were tended by priestesses known as vestals, and "to invest" referred to a process of becoming divinely centered in the earth.

According to Tacitus, all Europe regarded Mother Earth as the ruling deity, "to whom all else is subject and obedient," and it was believed all wisdom came directly from the land. Yet this ideal of the sacred had its horrifying aspects. To participate in the divine, men were required to imitate the women who once a month gave their "wise blood" to the fields.

In the spring, the earth was soaked in the blood of severed genitalia; later, the men were carried to the temple where they were anointed and solemnly buried in the Bridal Chamber. The initiates who survived this ritual dressed in women's clothes.

The rites of the matriarchy focused only on the part of the organic process in which the female body devours and absorbs. At planting time, a young man was killed and his body offered to the earth. It was believed that his blood would fertilize the land and bring about the resurrection of the crops. John the Baptist may have been one of these early vegetation kings. He was killed by an initiating priestess whose name was Salome. Her dance of the seven veils was part of the sacred drama celebrating our union with the earth. A male companion recently drew my attention to a Botticelli painting of this mythic scene. "This is how men feel," he said, pointing to the agonized expression on the prophet's face. "Can't you see this is *our* betrayal by the feminine?" It is no wonder that masculine cultures tried to keep their distance from the earth.

As women, we must own up to this wounding of the masculine. We cannot shift the blame for all our current woes to the oppression of the patriarchy. Instead, we must begin to recognize the potential for tyranny and oppression that reside within the female soul. Men have good reason to fear our authority. As a male friend, who is also a therapist, explained: "I feel uncomfortable myself when I am around a group of women who are conscious of their power. One part of me says this a wonderful thing. Yet another feels that something terrible is about to happen. I think, 'You'll bring me up, you'll have pride in me, and I'll be your sacrifice.'" In this myth, a man is required to give up everything, to deliver body and soul to some higher power that is wholly feminine. It is no simple matter for a woman to address this kind of suffering.

We find what seems to be a tremendous amount of violence directed toward the masculine in early European folklore and mythology. The people of northern Europe continued to offer up the vegetation king for several centuries. Villagers reenacted the castration of the god Loki, who fertilized the lap of the Goddess with his blood. In the Celtic world, a similar ritual was presided over by a goddess of flowers called Blodeuwedd, whose name suggests a bloody wedding. Her many spouses died to renew the earth, and she may have been the inspiration for the patriarchal tale of Bluebeard, in which the ritual slaying is reversed.

The idea of sacrifice appears again in the Middle Ages in the ceremony of knighthood. Here a young man who has been proven worthy receives a sword close to his neck, as if he were about to be ritually beheaded. Warfare may also have originated in our insistence that a man, too, must give his lifeblood to the earth. The warlike Mars was originally an Etruscan fertility god, and the Sufis worshiped a similar divinity known as *Maridyya*, from which we get the word *martyrdom*. Philosopher Sam Keen reminds us that men still offer up their bodies to placate the feminine. He urges women to meditate on the sacrifice of bodies in the last two major wars, saying, "We did this *for you.*"

While the body of the earth threatened to devour us, the body of a woman was seen as similarly overpowering. What was the role of the Goddess in the ancient world, if not to overwhelm us with her longing and desire? The poet Sappho said there was no greater tragedy than being separated from the lover's body. This is a strictly feminine point of view. In *Ego de Mono Katuedo,* Sappho mourns the space beside her in her bed:

> The Pleiades have set
> under the Westering moon,
> and I lie alone.

The trouble is that this goddess does not care who comes to fill the role. She is not concerned with permanence or with the uniqueness of her partner. Her desire is impersonal; it is a hunger for the renewal of the world. Eros lives in us and *through us,* and when confronted with this archetypal force, we are only secondary things.

Over the last two thousand years, we have tried to personalize our view of relationship. Yet from the beginning this shift was fraught with danger and with difficulty. By now, enough scholars have told the story: The new religions destroyed the Goddess to protect the individual from her collective rites. In the process, the earth was denigrated, marriage was forbidden, and sexuality condemned outright. The body was no longer a vehicle for communion with the living world; instead, it was a thing to be despised.

There were good reasons to create new customs and establish new religious rites: first, to do away with the tradition of male sacrifice. An old Babylonian rite involved the piercing of the body so the king's blood would fall in great drops and fertilize the earth. It was said, "If the king does not weep when struck, the omen is bad for the year." People believed the greater the victim's pain, the more fruit the earth would bear. Christianity set a limit to this suffering, and saved the world, not just for a year, but for all time. Yet it also rejected the amorous advances of the Goddess and, with this, the ideal of paradise. The word *Eden* means a "place of delight." Where the matriarchy proposed feasting and lovemaking in a tantalizing setting, the patriarchy preferred fasting in seclusion, far from the temptations of the flesh. Their headquarters were soon moved into the desert—a place where no life could grow and nothing need be fertilized.

Men also looked to the new religions to release them from the tyranny of domestic life. In the old-style marriages, property was held communally by the women, names of the children were taken from the mother, and men had no civil authority. In some tribes, it was possible for a wife to divorce her husband and leave him with nothing by staying away from their home for a period of three nights. Patriarchy brought about a mere reversal of these values; and too often the goal of "conversion" was to replace one kind of oppression with another.

Fig. 12 In matriarchal cultures, a woman was the guardian of the Tree of Life. With the advent of Christianity, that task was assigned to Eve, shown in this carving from the Cathedral of Saint-Lazare, Autun (central France).

A philosopher spoke out for reconciliation at the height of this bitter conflict. Simon Magus, a contemporary of Jesus, believed in the equality of the sexes and saw marriage as a path for spiritual development. Yet popular sentiment was against any such alliance at this time. For centuries, the only union to be formally recognized was the one between a true believer and his God. The Christian fathers managed to ignore the idea of marriage for quite some time. Astonishingly, it took some sixteen hundred years for the Church to sanctify the common-law relation between a husband and his wife.

While men and women have been divided into two opposing cultures, I am reminded that the word *religion* means "to bind together" and that our task is to somehow marry these two systems of belief. That is why we must begin to explore our common symbols and to look at the places where our two mythologies converge and overlap.

One image shared by both masculine and feminine religions is the Tree of Life (sees figures 12 and 13). In the matriarchies, the god who brought about the renewal of the crops was represented by a tree. This image can also be found in Christianity. I recently came upon a stained-glass window in a country chap-

Fig. 13 *Here Jesus is shown crucified upon the Tree of Life. This four-teenth-century painting by Simone dei Crocifissi is a reference to the eternal cycles of death and rebirth that rule the human spirit as well as the living world.*

el that portrayed the cross in this ancient aspect: attached to its base was an enormous root ball that was firmly planted in the ground—an assurance that masculine divinity is and must be anchored in the earth.

As Barbara Walker tells in the *Woman's Encyclopedia of Myths and Secrets*, the word *savior* also meant "he who plants the seed." In Christianity, the savior was the one who came to teach us about the "seeding" of the inner life. Christianity and the goddess religions are dependent on the same process of renewal, for the growth of the human spirit parallels the transformation of the natural world.

A divine child comes to bring about this miracle of redemption and rebirth, both in the early matriarchy and in Christian rites. Consider this description of the pagan ceremonies that took place at Eleusis. "Eleusis meant advent. Its principal rites brought about the advent of the Divine Child or Saviour, variously named Brimus, Dionysus, Triptolemus, Iasion, or Elenthereos, the Liberator. He was born of Demeter—the earth and laid in a manger or winnowing basket. His flesh was eaten by communicants in the form of bread made from the first or last sheaves. His blood was drunk in the form of wine. He entered the Earth and rose again. Communicants were supposed to partake of his immortality and after death they were known as blessed ones. . . . "

Pagan initiates entered a dark cave and were born again from the body of the Mother, while the Christian faithful hoped to rise up to the heavens and find new life with the Father. Our challenge today is to embrace both the figures as redeemers, to affirm that both masculine and feminine energies are necessary for the salvation of the world.

Today when I receive communion, I am reminded of our dark roots within the earth. I know that my energy flows in two directions: The spirit lifts me up, yet my bond with all creation pulls me down into the depths of life. This moment of tension—when we are suspended between the heavens and the natural world—is the heart of every liturgy. The great religions of the world have all been struggling to express this same organic truth. The poet Wendell Berry describes this process eloquently:

> It's the old ground trying it again.
> Solstice, seeding and birth—it never
> gets enough. It wants the birth of a man
> to bring together sky and earth, like a stalk of corn.
> It's not death that makes the dead
>   rise out of the ground,
> but something alive straining up,
>   rooted in darkness,
> like a vine.

The Brhadaranyaka Upanishad states it is our responsibility to reconcile the opposites. In the wedding ceremony, the husband says to his intended, "I am Heaven, Thou art Earth." In India, children listen to the stories of Radha and Krishna, two mythic beings whose marriage represents the union of matter and of consciousness. Young men are instructed in the arts of contemplation, while young women learn to create beauty and delight in every aspect of the home. This training goes on until a wedding date is set, and the ceremony is so elaborate it often lasts for a full three days. Those of us in the West have no tales of sacred lovers to explain the mystery of relationship—instead, we have the wisdom of the saints.

At first, I wondered how there could be any similarity between my own attempts to love and the inner battles of these holy men. Then I discovered that marriage is a container just like prayer or meditation, and that all relationships require fearless commitment and persistent faith.

Indeed, the trials the saint endures in his or her period of containment are not unlike the trials of married life. A relationship with God or with another person sends us into a kind of spiritual exile where we must confront our inner demons. These voices tell us a true union is impossible and intimacy cannot be trusted. I recall that, in the wilderness, Jesus was offered dominion over all the world if he would relinquish love. We, too, are tempted to choose power over union, to retreat into a world of our own creation in which we have full authority and control. This is the part of us that fears vulnerability and union, and would betray the energies of life.

As the poet Rilke said, the world is waiting for us to triumph over these fears and resistances and to leap out of the abyss and embrace the passion of the moment:

> Yes, the Spring had need of you. Many a star
> was waiting for you to espy it. Many a wave
> would rise on the past towards you;
>   or else, perhaps,
> as you went by an open window,
>   a violin would be giving
> itself to someone. All this was a trust.
> But were you equal to it?

The world holds out joy and bliss, but it is we who have such difficulty receiving it! At the very moment when a true union is possible, I may be overcome by fear, for meeting the beloved is as terrible as coming face to face with God. We have only to recall the warnings in the ancient myths: Actaeon was ravaged by his hounds when he dared to behold the goddess Artemis. Semele was annihilated when she asked to see the form of her beloved Zeus. No one dared to call upon the fiery presence of Jehovah or to even speak his name. With such stories to deter us, it is no wonder that we fear surrender to any power so much greater than ourselves.

Both the mystic and the lover must be bold enough to take this risk. They submit fully to the other, knowing there is no way out. This is the meaning of a vow or covenant. In *Marriage Dead or Alive,* the Jungian analyst Guggenbuhl-Craig writes,

"The life-long dialectical encounter between two partners, the bond of man and woman until death, can be understood as a special path for discovering the soul, [and] one of the essential features of this pathway is the absence of avenues for escape. Just as the saintly hermits cannot evade themselves, so the married person cannot avoid their partners."

Over and over we resist this bond because it involves this kind of confrontation, not only with our mates but with our own fears and anxieties. It has taken me many years to admit my secret dread—that, in the crucial moment, I would not be supported, that I would somehow be let down by life itself. Yet marriage is impossible if we do not have this basic trust. Twenty years ago I had a dream that illustrates this underlying fear of intimacy:

> I am in a subway station with my mother, watching a very feminine woman dressed in organdy like a bridesmaid. Suddenly the station shakes; the woman is being kidnapped, and her body is sent up a plastic tube to the other end of the station. Her head has been cut off, and a sign has been hung around her neck, which says, "sale merchandise."
>
> Now the people who have kidnapped her are after me. To survive, I have to fight in an arena. Beforehand I am supposed to make love to a young man with my opponent watching. At the end of the ritual, they are going to kill me. The bizarre thing is that I have to choose the man.
>
> I go into a room full of men and pick an innocent-looking youth. I tell him that I have to make love to him, and he responds, "Don't be afraid." I am not terrified of that, however, but of what might happen afterward.

At first, a bridesmaid is preparing for a marriage ceremony, but she has to do so underground. This is because marriage *is* a descent, a journey into darkness and uncertainty. It involves the whole person, even those hopes and aspirations that are still underground. This is a very ancient theme—one that goes back to the abduction of Persephone: in some sense, all women are in a similar plight. Our innocence must be stolen if we are to be initiated into the mysteries of life.

It was hard for me to feel confident, however, because in my dream the bridesmaid comes to such a bloody end. Right away, she is decapitated and her lifeless body turned into "sale merchandise." In my youth, there was no one to teach me the value of my own femininity. I had the notion that a loving relation could be bought; I saw people hire nurses and housekeepers in the belief that they could easily acquire the qualities of caring and compassion. My ideal of womanhood was in great danger just like the bridesmaid in the dream. The sexual act can only be one of capitulation—an opportunity to choose one's executioner—as long as the feminine principle is so dishonored.

The setting for the last part of the dream is an open arena, which recalls the collective nature of the marriage rite. I knew that union was something that the world required of me. Yet I experienced it as a violation because I did not have the proper strengthening. As a young woman, I was confused by a body of literature in which marriage is portrayed as annihilation, not a prelude to rebirth. I found this pessimism in the *liebestod,* or love-death, of the romantic myths. Consider the ill-fated ends of Romeo and Juliet, Tristan and Isolde. These lovers must be sacrificed because they have defied the rules of a given culture, and their passion is too intense. The message is that society is opposed to feeling. To surrender to love is to be cast out, to lose one's standing in the world.

Medieval Japanese society was so tradition-bound that lovers who crossed the social barriers had no other choice but suicide. They would find a high bridge, then tie themselves together and jump into the water. The practice was so widespread that it became the subject of an uneasy joke that is still told in modern-day Japan: A goldfish and a carp fell in love. Since they would not be allowed to marry, they decided to commit suicide. They tied themselves together—and then they jumped on land.

The joke is on us when we place these rules and regulations above our love for one another and our bond with life itself. Yet for centuries we have done precisely that. Marriages have been arranged for the purpose of maintaining wealth or creating alliances between families, and eros has been securely yoked to the demands and expectations of society. As a young woman, I merely asked the question that occupies each successive generation: Can I trust my own passion to break the bonds of the collective and lead me to a new experience of life?

Most cultures try to regulate both the passion and the terror that exist between the sexes. Under patriarchy, marriage became a controlled commodity to limit the powers of the feminine—largely because of our fear that the earth was a bloodthirsty female who demanded life and limb. Death itself was a woman in Sumerian tales, while the Hindus worshiped Kali as the great destroyer. At some point, however, the situation was reversed. In Greek mythology, the Underworld was ruled by a solitary god, and the Middle East soon produced a male deity with a thirst for bloodshed and revenge. These two mythologies are embedded in the unconscious and as a result, each sex now wears the death mask for the other.

There is this shadow aspect to every wedding, yet how are we to deal with it? How can we hope to enter marriage in such a terror-stricken state? Consider the dream I had just two weeks before my marriage:

> I am driving through the country, and a wedding is taking place. The bride is frightened and confused. She then looks down and sees blood on her white dress.

Clearly, the bride is being offered as a sacrifice. The fact is that marriage is, and always has been, connected to a host of bloody rites. There can be no wedding before the onset of the menses; blood is also involved in circumcision, which prepares the man for his wedding with the god. There is blood at the time of the ritual deflowering and blood during childbirth. In all these situations, blood has the power to redeem. There is an Arabic saying: Blood has flowed, the danger is past. René Girard writes in *Violence and the Sacred*, this is "the central idea of all sacrifice: that the offering appeases the powers and wards off the most severe chastisements which might otherwise befall." The shedding of blood releases tension, and the danger is transformed. We are no longer in the midst of a life-threatening situation but have come to a place of union and mutual support. Years later, I was able to acknowledge the teaching of this dream: In marriage, the blood is always mixed. There is wounding, and there is healing. This is the death and rebirth of the soul that is required in relationship.

Sacrifice may seem brutal and unnecessary, but in recoiling from the violence of it, we lose touch with the principles of life. Sacrifice is the key to renewal, and it is time to see it with new eyes. I know that the only way to amend a quarrel is to offer up some offending element within myself. This unity of consciousness is what our early rituals intended to achieve.

The world religions tell us that the death of the ego is necessary for our own inner growth, yet every advance of planetary life has required a like offering. From the very beginning, to eat and then be eaten was the way to liberate the energies of life. There was no birth that did not entail a death, while the survival of every animal depended on the sacrifice of another. This process is embedded in the very nature of the universe. Physicist Brian Swimme points out that the galaxy was created in such a sacrificial moment, beginning with the destruction of a star:

> Imagine that furnace out of which everything came
> forth. This was a fire that filled the universe—that

was the universe. There was no place free from it.
Every point of the cosmos was this explosion of
light and all the particles of the universe churned in
extremes of heat and pressure. This primeval fire-
ball burned for nearly a million years.

This all-consuming furnace produced the seed of life on
earth. People have honored this primordial sacrifice with can-
dles placed around their private altars and in creation stories
told around the sacred fire. All spiritual traditions acknowledge
that we are the survivors and benefactors of this fire, and to
participate in this everlasting ritual, our lives must burn as swift
and sure.

The writer Hermann Hesse reminds us that the individual is
the culmination of all other sacrifices:

I have already died all deaths,
And I am going to die all deaths again,
Die the death of the wood in the tree,
Die the stone death in the mountain,
Earth death in the sand,
Leaf death in the crackling summer grass
And the poor bloody human death.

Sacrifice does not *reduce* us to the level of the animals and
the grass. Rather it *expands* our consciousness until we become
one with all creation. It does not lead to our diminishment but
to our liberation—for as we make this offering, we discover
something new and different in ourselves. If we can approach
relationship this way, we will see that the aim is not subservi-
ence to another but the creation of a third identity. This is
perhaps why marriage is so difficult: to begin with, we must
surrender our need for control and certainty and give up a
portion of ourselves. The poet Wendell Berry knows that marriage is like entering a dark wood:

Sometimes our life reminds me
of a forest. . . .

The forest is mostly dark, its way
to be made anew day after day, the dark
richer than the light and more blessed
provided we stay brave
enough to keep on going in.

In the *Symposium,* Plato tells a story about the creation of the world in which there were no "others." In the beginning, all beings were hermaphroditic. Each possessed the masculine inventiveness of the god Hermes and the generative power of the goddess Aphrodite. Then one day these creatures were split asunder; they became male and female, and so human beings have been searching for their "lost half" ever since. Yet this longing has grown narcissistic; we do not look for our opposite but for a mirror image of ourselves. We can only be healed by what it is we lack, yet we steadily reject the cure!

The continuation of life depends on our ability to tolerate the unknown and unfamiliar. In mythology, this is regarded as the highest task. As Joseph Campbell has said, the hero is "someone who has given himself over to something other than himself. You can't think about your own protection, the journey is really about losing yourself, giving yourself to another." Yet such a thing can only be achieved once the ego is strong enough to give up the age-old fight for dominance.

C. G. Jung observed in his essay on analytical psychology, "Where love reigns, there is no will to power, and where the will to power is paramount, love is lacking. The one is but the shadow of the other." The drive for power comes from a fear that we will be swallowed by the other. It develops first as a defense against our childhood helplessness. But while its original purpose is to protect us, in the long run, it has the opposite effect, cutting us off from the people who could "complete us" and help us to reach out for love.

At one point in my marriage, I was in danger of giving in to this shadow and choosing control over love. The consequences were made clear to me in the following dream:

> I am talking to my mother, who has decided that
> she wants to die, that life is too difficult for her,
> that people can't be trusted and it is better to give
> up. I am struggling to remain uncontaminated by
> this flood of negative emotion while trying to con-
> sole her. I get off the phone because my husband
> and I are due at a counseling session, but he says
> not to bother coming—that he has something to
> work out with Delilah and that she is coming in my
> stead.

If we are still caught up in an ancient power struggle, we should not be surprised if a Delilah shows up in our dreams. Such a character represents the controlling feminine and connects us to the despair and negativity that have been handed down across the generations. My Delilah thinks that men have the advantages, that wives must be ruthless and deceitful, and women will not get the things they need. I was genuinely shocked when I discovered that I had given so much power to this inner archetype. Fear of the masculine—and fear of life—was transmitted so subtly and unconsciously that I was completely unaware I had taken over such beliefs.

This insinuating voice can generally be traced back to the disappointments of our parents, and it is important to review the patterns of control that have been taken over from our mothers and our fathers. When I first began this book, I consulted the *I Ching,* a twenty-five-hundred-year-old treatise on relationship. It sagely advised me to "work on what has been spoiled," referring to our traditional sex roles. This document says constructive action depends on the proper balancing of masculine and feminine and on knowing what behavior is authentic to ourselves. One commentary advises us to give up old patterns of control: "Often a father spends money without reference to his family's needs because his father did it; or, a wife uses devices to control her husband because her mother did it. We must reject such ideas as unworthy," says the *I Ching*. In short, we must begin to reinvent ourselves.

It might help if we could begin to see our relationships as objectively as we have seen the earth itself. Something very special occurred when the crew of the Apollo 7 beamed back a photograph of the planet from a distance of some two-hundred-thousand miles. This vision inspired both awe and wonder and enabled us to comprehend the basic unity of life.

Some years later a group of scientists carried this exploration one step further. They launched a space capsule filled with ordinary tools and objects to make our lives accessible to any intelligent beings in the far reaches of the galaxy. One critic said, "This information could prove more dangerous to us than any military codes passed on to enemy spies." Yet self-exposure was just the point. The capsule was an act of trust, a gesture based on the fundamental idea of reciprocity. It was an attempt to give back to the cosmos something akin to what the cosmos had given us: a sense of intimacy, a revelation, an unveiling. We must learn to honor this kind of reciprocity in all of our relationships, for we are being called, as never before, to risk and to reveal ourselves.

At the beginning of this century, the poet Federico García Lorca wrote,

> The rose
> was not searching for darkness or for science
> borderline of flesh and dream
> it was searching for something else.

We will find that "something else" when we learn to surrender to the longing for change that is built into the body of the world. In every moment of our lives, we somehow feel this push toward transformation. As we are formed in the womb, we sprout fins and gills and winglike appendages, as though we might be gathering the means to soar up to the heavens and dive deep into the earth. We are, from the very start, engaged in a reconciliation, a summing of all that has gone before.

This process continues on the psychological plane as we learn to embrace "the other" and surrender to the living world. Wendell Berry has said, "A man . . . is drawn to the wilderness much as he is drawn to a woman. It is, in its way, his opposite. It is as far as possible unlike his home or his work or anything he will ever manufacture. For that reason, he can take from it a solace—an understanding of himself such as he can find nowhere else." Here, then, is the similarity between the lover and the landscape: As we surrender to them both, we are transported beyond our ordinary selves.

It is often difficult to enfold something completely "other," yet the fate of the earth depends on our ability to take that risk. We must find a way to open up to nature and identify with the rivers and the mountains, the forests, and the air we breathe. The environment is now in such a critical state that we can no longer resist this transformation out of fear and ignorance.

Several years ago, I dreamed that I was in the bedroom with my husband. All of a sudden the earth began to shake. A group of men were blasting away at the shale deposits in a nearby meadow. I turned to my husband and said, "We can't make love in these circumstances. The earth is being wounded, and it can't take it anymore." This dream is a warning. It says, "You are not just damaging the water and the soil. You are damaging all of your relationships. You need to make a new commitment to the energies of life."

Each day, I remind myself that we are not here to control the environment, but to learn the lessons of humility and surrender. When I am capable of that, my life takes on a wholly different meaning. I no longer feel so small and separate. It is as though I am being held by a power that is both infinitely great and infinitely tender. My love for my husband and family does not exist in isolation; rather it is supported and enriched by my love for this world. This kind of trust is not something of our own creation, it comes to us in a moment of extraordinary grace. Just before he died, the poet Raymond Carver spoke about that gift:

> And did you get what
> you wanted from this life, even so?
> I did.
> And what did you want?
> To call myself beloved, to feel myself
> beloved on the earth.

———————————— ————————————

As I finish this book, the world is entering a whole new cycle. It is spring in the Hudson Valley and the earth is waking up. The ground is soft and waterlogged, and the top layer of the soil breaks open like the soft skin of a grape. I am intoxicated by a thousand different smells of mud and there is a sweetness in the air as the earth proclaims its readiness to open and receive. I put down my pen and listen to the chatter of the blue jays and the soughing of the pines. The wind has an edge to it today; it briskly slaps the bushes and the trees as if to rouse them from their logy sleep. There is something magical about this time of year when nature asks us to participate in her own seeding and rebirth.

In this season, we all are celebrants, taking part in nature's liturgy. For once, we do not try to impose our laws upon the landscape. Instead we allow ourselves to be enfolded by the earth's own process of creation. As I think back to the time when men and women lay down in the fields to call forth the fertility of the land, I, too, feel a new commitment to my marriage and to the preservation of the world.

On a clear Sunday afternoon recently, my husband and I walked through the Hurley cornfields and spoke about the difficulties we had weathered since last March. We had survived the usual batch of illnesses and family problems, and endured a three-month separation occasioned by my work. It had been a long, hard winter, and like the hard, insistent shoots sprouting through the earth, we, too, were ready to emerge from the darkness and stretch our spirits toward the light. We returned to our two-hundred-year-old farmhouse, built of stone and mud; we made new vows to one other. Later that day I wrote this poem about the way our love for one another is supported by the changes in the land:

This is the season of our turning.
The land is no longer desolate
        but open and inviting.
We are ready to take up our calling
        like two farmers
        bound together by the tilling of the fields.

We stand above the ready ground
        and fill it with our longing.
Here the seed is planted.
Here the earth is fed.
The rock is strong and holds us,
        even though it has been split.

This is the time for a new covenant.

We will watch the seasons pass
        aware of our own mortality
Trusting in the life which grows
        between us like an oak.

Marriage is this:
        a time for inward turning
        for mute and invisible growth.
It is also taking pleasure in each other
        until the love between us
        is embodied like a field.

BIBLIOGRAPHY

A Testament to the Wilderness: Ten Essays on an Address by C. A. Meier. Santa Monica, CA: Lapis Press, 1985.

Abbott, Franklin, ed. *New Men, New Minds: Breaking Male Tradition.* Freedom, CA: Crossing Press, 1987.

Berry, Adrian. See *Ideas about the Future,* edited by B. P. Beckwith, Palo Alto, CA: Beckwith. 1985.

Berry, Thomas. *The Dream of the Earth.* San Francisco: Sierra Club Nature and Natural Philosophy Library, 1988.

Berry, Wendell. *The Collected Poems of Wendell Berry.* San Francisco: North Point Press, 1985.

Budapest, Zsuzsanna. *The Holy Book of Women's Mysteries.* Oakland, CA: Susan B. Anthony Press, 1986.

Campbell, Joseph. *The Hero with a Thousand Faces.* Bollingen Series 17. Princeton, NJ: Princeton University Press, 1972.

Chernin, Kim. *Reinventing Eve.* New York: Harper & Row, 1988.

Chilton-Pearce, Joseph. *The Magical Child.* New York: Bantam New Age Books, 1981.

Cirlott, J. E. *A Dictionary of Symbols.* New York: Philosophical Library, 1971.

Dante Alighieri. *The Portable Dante.* Translated by Laurence Binyon. New York: Viking Press, 1947.

de Castillejo, Irene Claremont. *Knowing Woman.* New York: Harper & Row, 1974.

de Jong, H. M. E. *The Atalanta Fugiens of Michael Maier: Sources of an Alchemical Book of Emblems.* Leiden: E. J. Brill, 1969.

de Troyes, Chretien. *Yvain: Knight of the Lion.* Translated by Robert W. Ackerman and Frederick W. Locke. New York: Frederick Ungar Publishing, 1973.

Desmonde, William. *Magic, Myth and Money.* New York: Free Press of Glencoe, 1962.

Dillard, Annie. *An American Childhood.* New York: Harper & Row, 1987.

Downing, Christine. *The Goddess: Mythological Images of the Feminine.* New York: Crossroads, 1981.

Duncan, Robert. *The Opening of the Field.* New York: New Directions, 1960.

Eliade, Mircea. *Rites and Symbols of Initiation.* New York: Harper & Row, 1975.

Eliot, T. S. *Notes Towards the Definition of Culture.* New York: Harcourt, Brace & Company, 1949.

Frazer, Sir James. *The Golden Bough.* New York: Macmillan, 1922.

Frick, Thomas, ed. *The Sacred Theory of the Earth.* Berkeley, CA: North Atlantic Books, 1986.

Fromm, Erich. *The Anatomy of Human Destructiveness.* New York: Holt, Rinehart and Winston, 1973.

Fuentes, Carlos. *Terra Nostra.* New York: Farrar, Straus, Giroux, 1976.

Gide, André. *Oedipus and Theseus.* New York: Vintage Books, 1950.

Gimbutas, Marija. *Goddesses and Gods of Old Europe.* Berkeley, CA: University of California Press, 1982.

Giono, Jean. *Song of the World.* 1934. Reprint. San Francisco: North Point Press, 1980.

———. *Joy of Man's Desiring.* 1935. Reprint. San Francisco: North Point Press, 1981.

———. *The Man Who Planted Trees.* 1954. Reprint. Chelsea, VT: Chelsea Green Publishing, 1985.

Girard, René. *Violence and the Sacred.* Translated by Patrick Gregory. Baltimore: Johns Hopkins University Press, 1977.

Gorer, Geoffrey. See Alexander Mitscherlich, *Society without the Father.*

Grahn, Judy. *The Queen of Swords.* Boston: Beacon Press, 1987.

Graves, Robert. *The White Goddess.* Amended and enlarged edition. New York: Farrar, Straus, Giroux, 1966.

Griffin, Susan. *Woman and Nature: The Roaring Inside Her.* New York: Harper & Row, 1978.

Guggenbuhl-Craig, Adolf. *Marriage Dead or Alive.* Dallas: Spring Publications, 1977.

Guthrie, W. K. C. *The Greek Philosphers*. New York: Harper & Row, 1950.

Hamilton, Edith. *Mythology: Timeless Tales of Gods and Heroes*. New York: New American Library, 1969.

Hardy, Thomas. *Tess of the d'Urbervilles*. New York: New American Library, 1964.

Homer. *The Odyssey*. Translated by Robert Fitzgerald. New York: Doubleday, 1961.

Huxtable, Ada Louise. *Hello Hamburger, Goodbye History*. Washington, DC: Preservation Press, 1986.

I Ching or Book of Changes. Translated by Richard Wilhelm and Cary Baynes. Bollingen Series 19. Princeton, NJ: Princeton University Press, 1950.

Jacoby, Mario. *Longing for Paradise*. Boston: Sigo Press, 1985.

Johnson, Robert. *He: Understanding Masculine Psychology*. New York: Harper & Row, 1977.

Jung, C. G. "Anima and Animus." In *Aion: The Phenomenology of the Self*. Bollingen Series 20. Princeton, NJ: Princeton University Press, 1959.

_____. *Memories, Dreams, Reflections*. New York: Random House, Vintage Books, 1961.

_____. *The Collected Works*. Vol. 7, *Two Essays on Analytical Psychology*. Princeton, NJ: Princeton University Press, 1966.

Jung, C. G., and C. Kerenyi. *Essays on a Science of Mythology*. Bollingen Series 22. Princeton, NJ: Princeton University Press, 1969.

Jung, Emma, and Marie-Louise von Franz. *The Grail Legend*. Boston: Sigo Press, 1970.

Keillor, Garrison. *Lake Wobegon Days*. New York: Viking, 1985.

Kerenyi, C. *Eleusis: Archetypal Image of Mother and Daughter*. New York: Schocken Books, 1977.

Keuls, Eva C. *The Reign of the Phallus*. New York: Harper & Row, 1985.

Lawrence, D. H. *D. H. Lawrence: The Viking Portable Library*. New York: Viking, 1946.

Levertov, Denise. *Light up the Cave*. New York: New Directions, 1981.

Lincoln, Bruce. *Emerging from the Chrysalis*. Cambridge, MA: Harvard University Press, 1981.

Lowrie, Robert. *Primitive Religion*. New York: Liveright, 1970.

Luke, Helen. *Woman, Earth, and Spirit*. New York: Crossroads, 1981.

Mahdi, Louise Carus, Steven Foster, and Meredith Little, eds. *Betwixt and Between: Patterns of Masculine and Feminine Initiations*. LaSalle, IL: Open Court Books, 1987.

Mallory, William, and Paul Simpson-Housley, eds. *Geography and Literature*. Syracuse, NY: Syracuse University Press, 1987.

Markale, Jean. *Women of the Celts*. Translated by A. Mygind, C. Hauch, and P. Henry. Rochester, VT: Inner Traditions International, 1975.

Massey, Marilyn Chapin. *The Feminine Soul: The Fate of an Ideal*. Boston: Beacon Press, 1985.

Merchant, Carolyn. *The Death of Nature*. San Francisco: Harper & Row, 1980.

Mitscherlich, Alexander. *Society without the Father*. New York: Jason Aronson, 1973.

Monaco, Richard. *Parsival or a Knight's Tale*. New York: Macmillan, 1977.

Monick, Eugene. *Phallos: Sacred Image of the Masculine*. Toronto: Inner City Books, 1987.

Mookerjee, Ajit. *Kali: The Feminine Force*. London: Thames and Hudson, 1988.

Morey, Sylvester, and Olivia Gilliam, eds. *Respect for Life: The Traditional Upbringing of American Indian Children*. New York: Myrin Institute Books, 1974.

Mullahy, Patrick, ed. *Oedipus: Myth and Complex: A Review of Psychoanalytic Theory*. New York: Hermitage Press, 1948.

Munroe, Eleanor. *On Glory Roads: A Pilgrim's Book about Pilgrimage*. New York: Thames and Hudson, 1987.

Nahm, Milton, ed. *Selections from Early Greek Philosophy*. New York: Appleton, Century, Crofts, 1964.

Neumann, Erich. *The Great Mother*. Bollingen Series #47. Princeton, NJ: Princeton University Press, 1964.

Ovid: The Metamorphosis. Translated by Horace Gregory. New York: New American Library, 1958.

Pearson, Carol. *The Hero Within*. San Francisco: Harper & Row, 1986.

Perera, Sylvia Brinton. *Descent to the Goddess*. Toronto: Inner City Books, 1981.

Raglan, Lord. *The Hero*. New York: New American Library, 1979.

Rank, Otto. *The Trauma of Birth*. New York: Harcourt, Brace & Company, 1929.

Rawson, Philip. *The Art of Tantra*. New York: Oxford University Press, 1978.

Rilke, Rainer Maria. *The Duino Elegies*. Translated by J. B. Leishman and Stephen Spender. New York: W. W. Norton, 1963.

Rowan, John. *The Horned God: Feminism and Men as Wounding and Healing.* New York: Routledge & Kegan Paul, 1987.

Rush, Anne Kent. *Moon, Moon.* New York: Random House, 1976.

Sardello, Robert J., and Randolph Severson. *Money and the Soul of the World.* Dallas: Dallas Institute of Humanities and Culture, 1983.

Teilhard de Chardin, Pierre. *Building the Earth.* Denville, NJ: Dimension Books, 1965.

_____. *Hymn of the Universe.* New York: Harper & Row, 1969.

Thomas, Lewis. *Lives of a Cell: Notes of a Biology Watcher.* New York: Viking, 1974.

Tolstoy, Leo. *Anna Karenina.* Translated by David Magarshack. New York: New American Library, 1961.

Tournier, Michel. *Friday.* New York: Pantheon Books, 1969.

Turner, Victor. *The Ritual Process.* Ithaca, NY: Cornell University Press, 1977.

Uhlein, Gabriele, ed. *Meditations with Hildegard of Bingen.* Santa Fe, NM: Bear and Company, 1982.

von Franz, Marie-Louise. *The Feminine in Fairy Tales.* Zurich: Spring Publications, 1972.

_____. *Puer Aeternus.* Boston: Sigo Press, 1981.

von Kleist, Henrich. "Penthisilea." In *The Classic Theatre,* vol. 2, edited by Eric Bentley. New York: Doubleday Anchor, 1959.

Walker, Barbara. *The Woman's Encyclopedia of Myths and Secrets.* San Francisco: Harper & Row, 1983.

Williams, Daniel D. *Spirit and the Forms of Love.* Lanham, MD: Univeristy Press of America, 1981.

Wolkstein, Diane, and Noah Kramer. *Innana: Queen of Heaven and Earth.* New York: Harper & Row, 1983.

Woodman, Marion. *The Owl Was a Baker's Daughter: Anorexia Nervosa and the Repressed Feminine.* Toronto: Inner City Books, 1980.

_____. *Addiction to Perfection.* Toronto: Inner City Books, 1982.

_____. *The Pregnant Virgin: A Process of Psychological Transformation.* Toronto: Inner City Books, 1985.

Woolf, Virginia. *To the Lighthouse.* New York: Harcourt, Brace & Company, 1927.

Yi-Fu Tuan. *The Good Life.* Madison, WI: University of Wisconsin Press, 1986.

Young-Eisendrath, Polly. *Hags and Heroes*. Toronto: Inner City Books, 1984.

Yourcenar, Marguerite. *Fires*. New York: Farrar, Straus, Giroux, 1981.

Zimmer, Heinrich. *The King and the Corpse*. Edited by Joseph Campbell. Bollingen Series 11. Princeton, NJ: Princeton University Press, 1971.

INDEX

---

* Italicized page numbers refer to illustrations.

237

FIGURES:

1. A withered forest in Hawaii, photo © Robert A. Isaacs, Photo Researchers, Inc. Giacometti, *La forêt (7 figures et une tête),* 1950, bronze, Kunsthaus, Zurich. Photo courtesy of Laurie Platt Winfrey, Inc.

2. Cancer and the planet. (Left) photo © Tom McHugh, Photo Researchers, Inc. (Right) photo © M. Abbey, Photo Researchers, Inc.

3. Kiva, photo © David Hiser, Photographers/Aspen

4. Drawings on drum head, National Museum of Denmark, Copenhagen

5. Shaman's mask reproduced from *Dreams: Visions of the Night* by David Coxhead and Susan Hiller, London: Thames and Hudson, n.d.

6. Goddess figure and bowl, Koszta József Museum, Szentes, Hungary. Photos courtesy of Marija Gimbutas. Hedge maze and Cathedral floor plan from "Labyrinths," by Rosemary Jeanes, *Parabola,* vol. IV, no. 2, May 1979, pp. 14–15.

7. Mazes. (Top) © Denver Art Museum. (Lower left and right) from "Labyrinths," by Rosemary Jeanes, *Parabola,* vol. IV, no. 2, May 1979, pp. 12–13.

8. Terracotta figurine, National Museum of Anthropology, Mexico City. Photo courtesy of Laurie Platt Winfrey, Inc.

9. Stone Age sculptures of the Mother. (Top left) Leningrad Museum. (Top right) Hittite Museum, Ankara. (Lower left) Moldavian Museum. (Lower right) National Museum, Cagliari. All reproduced courtesy of Newsweek Books/Laurie Platt Winfrey, Inc.

10. Temple at Delos and phalli. (Top left) courtesy of the author. (Top right) History Museum, Romania. (Center) Grotte du Pape, *Horizon Search for Early Man,* p. 107. (Bottom) from *Eternal Present* by S. Giedion, 1962, p. 197. Reproduced with permission of Achille Wieder, Zurich, Switzerland. Photo courtesy of Laurie Platt Winfrey, Inc.

11. The Cerne Giant, photo © Marilyn Bridges, 1985. Reproduced courtesy of Felicia C. Murray.

12. Carving from Cathedral of Saint-Lazare, photo © Giraudon/Art Resource

13. Simone dei Crocifissi, Jesus crucified upon the Tree of Life, Pinacoteca, Bologna. Photo © Antonio Guerra.